Original title: Secrets of the NBA : Legendary Plays

© Secrets of the NBA : Legendary Plays, Carlos Martínez Cerdá and Víctor Martínez Cerdá, 2024

Authors: Víctor Martínez Cerdá and Carlos Martínez Cerdá (V&C Brothers)

© Cover and illustrations: V&C Brothers

Layout and design: V&C Brothers

All rights reserved.

This publication may not be reproduced, stored, recorded, or transmitted in any form or by any means, whether mechanical, photochemical, electronic, magnetic, electro-optical, by photocopying, or information retrieval systems, or any other current or future method, without prior written permission from the copyright holders.

SECRETS OF THE NBA
Legendary Plays

1

Shaquille O'Neal, one of the most dominant players in NBA history, is known for his great size, strength, and ability to dominate the game near the basket.

However, throughout his professional career, he only managed to score a three-point shot on one single occasion.

This fact is notable due to the unusualness of a player of his caliber and stature (2.16 meters and over 140 kg) scoring from that distance, as his game was primarily focused in the paint, where his physical advantage made him unstoppable.

O'Neal's only three-pointer occurred on February 16, 1996, during a game between the Orlando Magic and the Milwaukee Bucks.

In the final seconds of the game, with a large lead in favor of the Magic, O'Neal took a three-point shot, which ended up going in.

This three-pointer was celebrated by both his teammates and fans, as it was a rare event to see Shaq, a player known for his physical game near the basket, score from long distance.

Even though O'Neal wasn't known for his outside shooting ability, his career is filled with impressive achievements.

He won four NBA championships (three with the Los Angeles Lakers and one with the Miami Heat) and was named the league MVP in 2000.

His scoring average throughout his career was 23.7 points per game, and in his best season (1999-2000), he averaged 29.7 points per game.

However, when it comes to three-point shooting, his NBA career is notably unusual, as centers like him rarely move far from the basket.

In an interview, Shaquille O'Neal mentioned that he often played at 30% of his potential and didn't always give 100% on the court.

This statement was controversial, as many wondered how much greater his impact could have been if he had consistently played at his maximum potential.

Despite this, his presence on the court was dominant, and his playing style, which combined brute strength with surprising agility for a player of his size, made him an NBA icon.

Throughout his career, O'Neal faced various criticisms for his off-court lifestyle, his struggles with free throws, and the perception that he wasn't always in top physical shape.

However, his impact on basketball is undeniable.

He was a 15-time All-Star, a three-time NBA Finals MVP, and his number has been retired by both the Lakers and the Miami Heat, teams with which he left an indelible mark.

2

The 2000 NBA Draft is widely regarded as one of the worst in the league's history.

Held on June 28 of that year, it left much to be desired in terms of overall talent, with most of the selected players failing to meet the expectations typically associated with an NBA draft.

This draft stands out for its lack of impactful players, low statistical performance, and scarcity of emerging stars.

Unlike other drafts that have produced multiple All-Star players, the 2000 draft was notable for the near-total absence of stars.

Of the 58 players selected, only Kenyon Martin, chosen first overall by the New Jersey Nets, became an All-Star, and he only achieved this once, in 2004.

This lack of star talent is one of the main reasons why this draft is viewed so negatively.

Many of the selected players failed to establish long or successful careers in the NBA.

Several of them struggled to stay in the league, and those who did failed to achieve significant performance.

Players like Stromile Swift (second pick), Darius Miles (third pick), and Marcus Fizer (fourth pick) never lived up to the expectations associated with their draft positions.

The overall statistics of the selected players were mediocre, as few managed to average significant numbers in points, rebounds, assists, or other important statistical categories, which strongly contrasted with other drafts that, even with lower picks, produced players who left a mark on the league.

Beyond Kenyon Martin, most of the first-round picks were disappointing.

Even players selected later, like Jerome Moiso and Courtney Alexander, had careers that quickly faded.

To put into perspective how disappointing the 2000 draft was, it is enough to compare it with other famous drafts, such as the 1984 draft, which produced Michael Jordan, Hakeem Olajuwon, and Charles Barkley, or the 1996 draft, which brought Kobe Bryant, Allen Iverson, and Steve Nash.

Even the 1986 draft, which is also considered one of the worst due to the personal tragedies and failures of some players, had a greater impact than the 2000 draft.

The 2000 Draft took place during a time when the NBA was in transition, with many stars from the 1990s nearing the end of their careers, which increased the pressure on the new players to take over, but unfortunately, the class of 2000 did not live up to expectations.

The lack of success of this draft class underscored the importance of scouting and player development, leading the league to review and improve its talent evaluation methods.

Although some players had respectable careers, like Kenyon Martin, Hedo Turkoglu, and Jamal Crawford, the class as a whole did not meet expectations.

Not only did the players selected fail to reach star status, but many also struggled to stay in the league for several years.

3

Both Gerald Green and Davis Bertans, two recognized basketball players, share a curious and remarkable characteristic: they both have only nine fingers, having lost the ring finger on their right hand in accidents that occurred during their childhood.

Despite this disability, both have managed to stand out in professional basketball, defying expectations and proving that physical limitations have not been an obstacle to their success in the sport.

Gerald Green, a former NBA player known for his athleticism and spectacular dunks, lost his finger at the age of 11.

The accident happened when Green was attempting a dunk on a basket at his home.

Unfortunately, the basket's support had an exposed nail on the edge, and his right ring finger got caught on it.

As a result, his finger was severely torn, and the doctors had no choice but to amputate it.

Despite the severity of the accident, Green didn't let this stop him.

He developed his talent and became a notable player, especially known for winning the NBA Slam Dunk Contest in 2007.

His NBA career spanned several teams, and he is remembered for his impressive ability to soar through the air, despite the loss of his finger.

On the other hand, Davis Bertans, a Latvian player currently active in the NBA, lost his right ring finger when he was 13 years old.

The accident occurred while he was chopping wood. Bertans was using a saw when his glove got caught, causing the saw to cut his ring finger in half.

Despite this traumatic injury, Bertans continued pursuing his dream of playing professional basketball.

Known for his shooting ability, especially from the three-point line, Bertans has had a successful NBA career, standing out for his shooting accuracy and his ability to overcome the physical limitations imposed by the loss of his finger.

What is impressive about both players is not just their ability to play at the highest level with a physical disability, but also how they have adapted their games to leverage their strengths.

In Green's case, his ability to perform spectacular dunks is even more astonishing considering the absence of a finger on his dominant hand.

As for Bertans, his prowess as an elite shooter is a testament to his determination and his ability to perfect his technique despite the loss of a finger on his shooting hand.

4

Stephen Curry, the superstar of the Golden State Warriors, is widely recognized as the best three-point shooter in NBA history.

His ability to shoot from long range has revolutionized the game, and he has set multiple records in the league, including the most three-pointers made.

Curry reached a significant milestone in his career when he surpassed 3,000 three-pointers, becoming the first player in NBA history to achieve this mark.

This accomplishment occurred on December 28, 2021, during a game against the Denver Nuggets.

Throughout his career, Curry has redefined what it means to be a shooter in the NBA.

His ability to hit three-pointers from anywhere on the court, often from positions that were previously considered irrational, has forced teams to rethink their defenses and has changed the way basketball is played at both professional and amateur levels.

His influence extends beyond his statistics, as he has inspired a new generation of players to prioritize the three-point shot as a primary offensive tool.

The game in which Curry reached the 3,000 three-pointers did not end in a victory for the Warriors, as they were defeated by the Denver Nuggets 89-86.

Although the celebration of Curry's personal achievement was subdued by the loss, this milestone underscores his consistency and longevity as an elite shooter.

Throughout his career, Curry has broken several three-point shooting records, including the most three-pointers in a single season and the most three-pointers in a playoff game.

Curry's career has been marked by his ability to elevate the level of play of his team.

Under his leadership, the Golden State Warriors have won multiple NBA championships and set a new standard for success based on the efficiency and volume of three-point shooting.

His impact on the league is undeniable, and his three-point record is a testament to his unique skill and dedication to the sport.

5

Manute Bol and Muggsy Bogues are two of the most iconic players in NBA history, not only for their skills on the court but also for their physical characteristics, which placed them at the opposite extremes of the height spectrum in basketball.

Manute Bol, with an astonishing height of 2.31 meters (7'7"), was one of the tallest players in NBA history.

On the other hand, Tyrone "Muggsy" Bogues, nicknamed "The Flea," stood at just 1.60 meters (5'3"), making him the shortest player in the history of the league.

Despite this height difference, the two were teammates during the 1987-1988 season with the Washington Bullets, forming one of the most mismatched pairs ever seen in the NBA.

The height difference between Manute Bol and Muggsy Bogues is 71 centimeters (28 inches), an impressive disparity that symbolizes the extreme contrasts that can exist in a sport like basketball, where height is usually a determining factor.

Manute Bol, originally from Sudan, was known for his shot-blocking ability, averaging 3.3 blocks per game throughout his career.

His presence on the court was intimidating due to his enormous wingspan, and his defensive ability was a valuable asset for any team.

Bol was a unique figure, not only for his height but also for his dedication to humanitarian causes, using his fame to support his native country.

On the other hand, Muggsy Bogues defied all expectations typically associated with a professional basketball player due to his height.

Despite standing at just 1.60 meters (5'3"), Bogues was an exceptionally fast and skilled point guard, with court vision and a knack for stealing the ball that made him stand out.

His speed and agility allowed him to compete against much taller and stronger players, and his leadership on the court made him a cornerstone for the teams he played for, especially the Charlotte Hornets, where he found the most success.

When Bol and Bogues played together on the Washington Bullets, the sight of the two of them on the court captured the imagination of fans.

The remarkable height difference between the two players became a recurring topic in the media, and their photos together remain some of the most iconic of the era.

Their time as teammates on the Bullets was relatively short, but it left a lasting mark on NBA history, symbolizing that success in basketball can come in all shapes and sizes.

6

The retirement of NBA players is a complex issue that, unfortunately, is often associated with significant financial and personal difficulties.

According to a report by Sports Illustrated published several years ago, approximately 60% of NBA players end up financially ruined within five years of retiring from professional basketball.

This alarming percentage highlights the challenges many former players face in adjusting to life after the sport and the poor management of the fortunes they accumulate during their careers.

The reasons why so many players end up in precarious financial situations after retirement are numerous.

Many players come from disadvantaged backgrounds and, when receiving large sums of money at a young age, often lack the financial education needed to manage them properly.

Moreover, the lifestyle they lead during their careers—marked by high expenses on luxury goods, cars, jewelry, properties, and entertainment—often proves unsustainable in the long term, especially when income from contracts and sponsorships decreases or disappears entirely after their careers end.

Another contributing factor is the pressure from friends, family, and associates who often depend on them financially, which can lead to irresponsible investments or loans that are never repaid.

Among the most well-known players who have faced serious financial problems after retirement are Dennis Rodman, Allen Iverson, Antoine Walker, and Latrell Sprewell.

Dennis Rodman, famous for his defensive play and eccentric personality, earned millions during his NBA career, especially during his time with the Chicago Bulls, where he was a key part of their success in the 1990s.

However, after retiring, Rodman encountered serious financial troubles due to his extravagant lifestyle, legal issues, and difficulties maintaining the same level of income he had during his career.

Rodman has made headlines several times for his inability to pay child support and other debts.

Allen Iverson, known as "The Answer," was one of the most electrifying players in the NBA and a cultural icon during his time in the league.

He earned over $200 million throughout his career, including his contracts and endorsements, yet Iverson faced financial problems after his retirement, partly due to an expensive lifestyle and poor investment decisions.

It was reported that he struggled to pay his debts and maintain his previous lifestyle, although a trust fund created by Reebok, which will be released when he turns 55, could provide him with some financial stability in the future.

Antoine Walker, a three-time All-Star and NBA champion with the Miami Heat in 2006, is another example of a player who experienced extreme financial difficulties after his career ended.

Walker earned around $108 million during his time in the NBA, but he declared bankruptcy in 2010, just two years after retiring.

The reasons included reckless spending, failed investments, and a large amount of loans and debts that he was unable to pay.

Latrell Sprewell, known for his talent on the court and his controversial behavior, also faced financial problems after his NBA career.

Sprewell turned down a $21 million contract with the Minnesota Timberwolves in 2004, claiming it was insufficient to support his family.

Years later, it was reported that he had lost most of his fortune, facing foreclosure on his properties and the seizure of his yacht.

7

The history of the Portland Trail Blazers in the NBA Draft is marked by two of the most unfortunate decisions in league history, decisions that, in hindsight, had a significant impact on the franchise's trajectory.

In 1984, the NBA Draft was one of the most talented of all time, producing stars like John Stockton and Charles Barkley.

However, the top three prospects were two centers and a guard: Hakeem Olajuwon, Sam Bowie, and Michael Jordan.

With the first pick, the Houston Rockets selected Olajuwon, a decision that proved successful as he led the team to two NBA championships.

The Portland Trail Blazers, holding the second pick, chose Sam Bowie, a center from the University of Kentucky.

Although Bowie had a respectable career, playing five years with Portland and averaging solid numbers, he is most remembered for being picked ahead of Michael Jordan, who was selected third by the Chicago Bulls.

Jordan, of course, went on to become one of the greatest basketball players of all time, winning six championships with the Bulls and revolutionizing the sport on a global scale.

The choice of Sam Bowie over Michael Jordan has been criticized for decades and is viewed as one of the biggest "blunders" in NBA Draft history.

Part of the reason Portland chose Bowie was that they already had a talented guard in Clyde Drexler and needed to strengthen the center position.

However, Bowie's leg injuries severely limited his potential, while Jordan quickly ascended to stardom.

Years later, in 2007, Portland had another chance to change their fortunes when they secured the first overall pick in the draft.

The decision came down to Greg Oden, a dominant center from Ohio State University, and Kevin Durant, a talented forward from the University of Texas.

Portland selected Oden, a decision that many at the time considered logical since Oden was viewed as a generational prospect at the center position.

However, Oden struggled with chronic injury issues, mainly in his knees, which limited his career to just 105 NBA games before retiring in 2014.

On the other hand, the then Seattle Supersonics (later becoming the Oklahoma City Thunder) selected Kevin Durant with the second pick.

Durant went on to become one of the greatest players of his generation, winning multiple scoring titles, an NBA MVP award, and two championships with the Golden State Warriors.

The choice of Oden over Durant is seen as another major draft mistake, comparable to Bowie over Jordan.

These two draft decisions have haunted the Portland Trail Blazers for years, especially as the franchise continues to search for its first championship since 1977.

The narrative of "what could have been" is a recurring theme in Portland's history, and although the franchise has had moments of success since then, they have never been able to replicate the dominance they might have achieved if they had selected Jordan in 1984 or Durant in 2007.

The Blazers' draft history serves as a reminder of how unpredictable and crucial the selection process can be in the NBA, where even the most informed decisions can have unexpected and long-lasting results.

8

The 1996 NBA Draft is one of the most memorable and talented in the league's history, but it's also notable for the fact that 13 teams overlooked the opportunity to select Kobe Bryant, who would go on to become one of the greatest players in basketball history.

Kobe Bryant was selected 13th overall by the Charlotte Hornets, a team that, in a move that seems incomprehensible to many today, decided to trade him to the Los Angeles Lakers in exchange for veteran center Vlade Divac.

Kobe Bryant, a young prodigy who had just graduated from Lower Merion High School in Philadelphia, was not initially seen as a sure bet by many teams, partly due to the uncertainty of selecting a player who had not played college basketball.

At that time, it was uncommon for players to jump directly from high school to the NBA, and many teams preferred to select players with college basketball experience.

This explains why so many teams chose other players before Bryant.

The players selected before Kobe Bryant included Allen Iverson, who was the first overall pick by the Philadelphia 76ers and had a stellar career, and other notable players like Marcus Camby, Stephon Marbury, Ray Allen, and Antoine Walker, who also had successful careers in the NBA.

However, some of the players chosen before Bryant, such as Todd Fuller, Vitaly Potapenko, and Samaki Walker, never reached superstar status.

The trade between the Charlotte Hornets and the Los Angeles Lakers was largely facilitated by Jerry West, then general manager of the Lakers, who had identified Bryant's potential early on.

West saw in Bryant a unique talent and convinced the Hornets to make the trade, knowing that the Lakers needed a center to replace Divac and that Charlotte was seeking an interior presence.

What the Hornets didn't know at the time was that they were giving away one of the players who would redefine the NBA over the next two decades.

Kobe Bryant went on to play 20 seasons with the Los Angeles Lakers, winning five NBA championships, two Finals MVP awards, and one regular-season MVP in 2008.

He was an 18-time All-Star and left an indelible mark on NBA history, both for his talent on the court and his unmatched work ethic, often referred to as the "Mamba Mentality."

The fact that 13 teams passed on Bryant serves as a reminder of how unpredictable the NBA Draft can be.

Teams often make decisions based on immediate needs or perceptions of a player's potential at the time, but the long-term impact of those decisions isn't always easy to foresee.

For the teams that passed on Bryant, it's a case of "what could have been," while for the Lakers, it was one of the best decisions in franchise history.

9

**The Boston Celtics and the New York Knicks are two
of the most historic and revered franchises in the NBA.**

Both founded in 1946, these teams are not only some of the oldest in the league, but they also stand out for their stability, having never changed their names or cities since their inception.

This continuity has allowed both franchises to build strong identities and establish themselves as cornerstones in the history of professional basketball.

The Boston Celtics are synonymous with success in the NBA.

Since their founding, the Celtics have accumulated a total of 17 NBA championships, tying with the Los Angeles Lakers for the most titles in league history.

The Celtics' most dominant era occurred in the 1950s and 1960s under the leadership of legendary coach Red Auerbach.

During that time, the Celtics won 11 championships in 13 years, led by iconic players such as Bill Russell, Bob Cousy, and John Havlicek.

The Celtics' influence on the NBA goes beyond their championships; they set a standard of excellence in teamwork and defense, characteristics that defined the franchise's identity for decades.

In the 1980s, the Celtics experienced a second golden era with the arrival of Larry Bird, who, along with Kevin McHale and Robert Parish, formed one of the most formidable trios in NBA history.

This era was marked by the intense rivalry with Magic Johnson's Los Angeles Lakers, resulting in one of the most legendary competitions in sports, which helped elevate the profile of the NBA worldwide.

Throughout their history, the Celtics have maintained a strong cultural identity and have been a team that represents Boston's competitive and winning spirit.

On the other hand, the New York Knicks also have a rich history and a prominent place in the NBA, though with less success compared to the Celtics.

The Knicks were one of the founding teams of the Basketball Association of America (BAA), which merged with the National Basketball League (NBL) in 1949 to form the modern NBA.

Throughout their history, the Knicks have been known for their passionate fan base and for playing in Madison Square Garden, one of the most iconic arenas in the world, often called "The Mecca of Basketball."

The Knicks reached their peak in the 1970s and 1990s.

In the 1970s, led by players like Willis Reed, Walt Frazier, and Dave DeBusschere, the Knicks won two NBA championships, in 1970 and 1973.

The 1970 title is particularly memorable for Willis Reed's heroic performance in Game 7 of the Finals, when, despite being injured, he took to the court and scored the first points, inspiring his team to victory over the Lakers.

In the 1990s, the Knicks, led by Patrick Ewing, became an elite team in the Eastern Conference, reaching the NBA Finals in 1994 and 1999.

However, although they came close, they were unable to win another championship, being defeated by the Houston Rockets in 1994 and the San Antonio Spurs in 1999.

Despite the lack of titles in recent decades, the Knicks remain one of the most valuable and popular franchises in the NBA, with a significant cultural presence and a history rich in tradition and unforgettable moments.

Both franchises, the Celtics and the Knicks, share a longevity and stability that few others in the NBA can match.

They have never changed cities or names, which has allowed both to develop and maintain a loyal fan base and a lasting legacy in the sport.

This stability has been key to their identity and has made them seen as the "guardians" of NBA tradition and history.

10

Muggsy Bogues and Manute Bol form one of the most unusual and memorable duos in NBA history, as they represented the extreme ends of height in professional basketball.

Standing at 1.60 meters (5'3"), Muggsy Bogues is the shortest player to ever play in the NBA, while Manute Bol, at 2.31 meters (7'7"), was one of the tallest players in the league's history.

Both shared the court as teammates on the Washington Bullets (now Washington Wizards) during the 1987-1988 season, creating an iconic image of physical contrast on the court.

Muggsy Bogues was selected by the Washington Bullets as the team's first pick in the 1987 Draft, following a standout college career at Wake Forest.

Despite his short stature, which initially caused many to doubt his ability to compete at the highest level, Bogues proved that size did not determine success in the NBA.

He was known for his speed, agility, and court vision, making him an exceptional point guard.

His ability to steal the ball and handle pressure were key elements of his game.

Throughout his 14-year NBA career, Bogues played for several teams, including the Charlotte Hornets, where he achieved his best performance.

One of Bogues' standout achievements was his average of 10.8 points per game during the 1993-1994 season with the Charlotte Hornets.

This season was one of the best of his career and demonstrated that, despite his height, he could be a key contributor on a competitive team.

Additionally, Bogues blocked 39 shots throughout his NBA career, a remarkable feat considering the significant height difference between him and most of the players he faced.

Manute Bol, on the other hand, was primarily known for his shot-blocking ability.

With his towering height of 2.31 meters (7'7") and an even more impressive wingspan, Bol became one of the best shot blockers in NBA history.

In his rookie season, he averaged 5.0 blocks per game, leading the league in that category.

Bol was an intimidating defensive presence, and his ability to alter shots in the paint made opponents think twice before attempting to score near him.

The sight of Muggsy Bogues and Manute Bol together on the court was a unique spectacle.

The 71-centimeter (28-inch) height difference between them emphasized the diversity of players who can succeed in the NBA, regardless of traditional physical attributes.

While Bol dominated on defense and was a shot-blocking specialist, Bogues excelled with his quickness, defensive skills, and leadership as a point guard.

Together, they represented the idea that basketball is a sport where talent and skill can overcome apparent physical limitations.

Throughout his career, Bogues continued to be a symbol of determination and perseverance, showing that height is not an insurmountable obstacle in basketball.

His legacy endures as an inspiring example for young players who dream of reaching the NBA, regardless of their size.

Manute Bol, for his part, also left a significant legacy, both on and off the court, being remembered not only for his defensive abilities but also for his humanitarian work and his commitment to his native country, Sudan.

11

The NBA logo is one of the most recognizable symbols in the world of sports.

The iconic white silhouette against a blue and red background that represents the league is, in fact, the stylized image of Jerry West, a legend of the Los Angeles Lakers.

Although it has not been officially confirmed by the NBA due to legal and image rights issues, it is widely known that West is the figure on which the logo is based, designed in 1969 by Alan Siegel.

Jerry West, nicknamed "Mr. Clutch" for his ability to perform under pressure, is considered one of the greatest players in NBA history.

During his 14-season career with the Lakers, West was an exceptional shooting guard and point guard, known for his precise shooting, ball-handling ability, and defensive prowess.

However, despite his outstanding skills, West is also sadly known for his unfortunate history in the NBA Finals.

West reached the NBA Finals nine times during his career, all with the Lakers.

However, he lost eight of those Finals, becoming the player who lost the most times in a championship series.

Most of his Finals losses came against the Boston Celtics during a time when the rivalry between the two teams was at its peak.

Despite his heroic performances, which included averaging 40.6 points per game in the 1965 Finals and being named Finals MVP in 1969 even though the Lakers lost that series, the championship always seemed to elude him.

Finally, in 1972, in his ninth appearance in the Finals, West and the Lakers broke the curse by defeating the New York Knicks in five games.

This title was particularly significant not only for West but for the entire Lakers team, which had set a record of 33 consecutive wins that season.

For West, winning that championship was the crowning moment of his career, putting an end to years of frustration and nearly a decade of Finals losses.

An interesting fact about the NBA logo is that the silhouette of West is holding the ball with his left hand, even though he was actually right-handed.

This detail has generated some intrigue over the years, but it also adds a unique touch to the league's emblem.

The choice of West as the inspiration for the logo was due to his fluid playing style, elegance on the court, and ability to represent basketball at its finest, encapsulating what the NBA wanted to project as the image of the sport.

Jerry West is not only the face behind the logo but also a symbol of perseverance and excellence in basketball.

His legacy extends beyond his time as a player; after retiring, he continued to influence the NBA as a coach, general manager, and executive, playing a crucial role in building championship teams like the Lakers and the Golden State Warriors.

12

Shaquille O'Neal and Kareem Abdul-Jabbar are two of the most dominant centers in NBA history, known for their ability to score near the basket, their imposing physical presence, and their ability to impact the game on both ends of the court.

Together, they boast nearly 40 years of experience in the league, with 20 seasons for Abdul-Jabbar and 19 for O'Neal.

Throughout their illustrious careers, they achieved numerous championships, MVP awards, and broke several records.

However, there is one area of the game where they did not excel: three-point shooting.

Despite their immense success, Shaquille O'Neal and Kareem Abdul-Jabbar each made only one three-pointer throughout their entire careers.

This may seem surprising in the modern era of basketball, where the three-point shot has become a central aspect of the game.

However, for most of O'Neal's and Abdul-Jabbar's careers, basketball was played very differently, with a much greater emphasis on interior play, especially for centers.

Kareem Abdul-Jabbar, who played in the NBA from 1969 to 1989, is the league's all-time leading scorer with 38,387 points.

Much of his scoring came from his signature "skyhook," an almost unstoppable hook shot that he executed with great accuracy from anywhere near the basket.

The three-point shot was not introduced to the NBA until the 1979-1980 season, by which time Abdul-Jabbar was already well into his career.

As a result, he never developed a three-point shot as part of his offensive arsenal.

His only three-pointer came during the 1986-1987 season, at a time when he was already a well-established veteran, and it was not a regular part of his game.

Shaquille O'Neal, who played in the NBA from 1992 to 2011, was equally dominant in the low post.

With his enormous size and strength, O'Neal became one of the hardest players to defend in NBA history.

His focus was on scoring near the basket, using his physique to overpower defenders and gain position under the hoop.

The three-point shot was never part of his game, and his only three-pointer occurred on February 16, 1996, during a game between the Orlando Magic and the Milwaukee Bucks.

It was an unusual shot taken in the final seconds of the game when the Magic had already secured the victory.

Both players, despite their limited ability to score from long range, redefined what it means to be a dominant center in the NBA.

The lack of three-pointers in their statistics does not diminish their impact on the game; in fact, it highlights the specialization and effectiveness both had in their roles.

During their eras, centers were not expected or required to shoot threes; their primary job was to dominate the paint, protect the rim, and secure rebounds.

Both Abdul-Jabbar and O'Neal excelled in these areas and built historic careers based on their ability to score, defend, and lead their teams from the paint.

In today's NBA, where the three-point shot is a crucial part of the game for almost every position, it's interesting to reflect on how players like O'Neal and Abdul-Jabbar might have evolved in a different context.

However, their legacy remains untarnished, and their contributions to basketball are immense.

Their careers highlight that while the game has changed over time, the ability to dominate in the low post and exert physical influence on the game remains a valuable attribute, even if that dominance doesn't include the three-point shot.

13

On December 17, 1991, the Cleveland Cavaliers made history by setting the record for the largest margin of victory in an NBA game, defeating the Miami Heat by an overwhelming 68 points, with a final score of 148 to 80.

This result remains, to date, the most dominant victory in terms of point differential in league history.

The game took place at the Richfield Coliseum, the former home of the Cavaliers. From the start, Cleveland displayed overwhelming superiority on both ends of the court.

The Cavaliers dominated the first quarter, scoring 42 points while the Heat managed only 23 in response.

As the game progressed, the point differential continued to increase dramatically.

The Cavaliers, led by key players like Mark Price, Brad Daugherty, Larry Nance, and Craig Ehlo, were relentless throughout the game.

Their fluid offense and suffocating defense left Miami struggling to find any rhythm.

The Heat, a relatively new team in the NBA at the time (founded in 1988), had no answer for the level of execution displayed by the Cavaliers.

In that game, the Cavaliers shot with 57.8% accuracy from the field, an impressive percentage that underscored their offensive dominance.

Additionally, the Cleveland team dished out a total of 39 assists, highlighting their excellent ball movement and on-court cohesion.

On the other hand, Cleveland's defense held the Heat to just 80 points, with a poor 35.1% shooting from the field.

The Heat, led by coach Kevin Loughery, had no answers offensively or defensively.

Throughout the game, Miami was unable to find their rhythm, and their attempts to narrow the gap were quickly neutralized by the Cavaliers.

In the end, the scoreboard reflected a 68-point difference, setting a record that still stands more than three decades later.

This result was a reflection of the Cavaliers' strength during that season, in which they finished with a solid 57-25 record, securing third place in the Eastern Conference.

Despite their success in the regular season, the Cavaliers were eliminated in the conference semifinals by Michael Jordan's Chicago Bulls, who went on to win the championship.

On the other hand, the Heat finished the season with a 38-44 record, barely making the playoffs, where they were eliminated in the first round by the Chicago Bulls.

The game against the Cavaliers remained a painful reminder of the challenges the team faced in their early years in the league.

This game is remembered not only for the magnitude of the victory but also as a testament to the unpredictability of basketball.

14

In the history of the NBA, the Draft is one of the most highly anticipated events, as it allows franchises to select new talent that could transform their teams.

Having the first overall pick in the Draft is a privilege often associated with the opportunity to select a generational player who can change the direction of a franchise.

However, there are six teams in the NBA that have never had the chance to select first overall, which is rare in a league where a team's fate can change dramatically with a single pick.

The six franchises that have never selected first are:

1. Denver Nuggets: Founded in 1967 as the Denver Rockets in the ABA, the Nuggets joined the NBA in 1976 after the leagues merged. Despite being a competitive team for much of their history, they have never had the first overall pick in the Draft. The Nuggets have built strong teams through lower picks, trades, and player development, as in the case of Nikola Jokić, an NBA MVP selected in the second round in 2014.

2. Indiana Pacers: The Pacers, also founded in the ABA in 1967 and then integrated into the NBA in 1976, are another franchise that has never selected first. Throughout their history, Indiana has been a consistent playoff team but has never fallen low enough in the standings to secure the first overall pick.

Despite this, they have been successful in selecting players like Reggie Miller, who became a team legend after being selected 11th overall in 1987.

3. Memphis Grizzlies: They began as an expansion franchise in Vancouver in 1995 before relocating to Memphis in 2001. Despite being a relatively young franchise, the Grizzlies have had multiple opportunities in the Draft lottery but have never secured the first pick. Their highest selection was second in 2009, when they selected Hasheem Thabeet, a move that did not work out as expected. However, their selection of Ja Morant with the second pick in 2019 has been a resounding success.

4. Miami Heat: Since their founding in 1988, the Miami Heat have become one of the most successful franchises in the NBA, winning three championships. However, they have never had the first overall pick in the Draft. Miami's success has been built through smart Draft decisions, key free agents like LeBron James and Chris Bosh, and a winning culture established by Pat Riley. Their highest pick was second in 2008, when they selected Michael Beasley.

5. Oklahoma City Thunder (formerly Seattle SuperSonics): Founded in 1967, they became the Oklahoma City Thunder in 2008. Although the SuperSonics selected Kevin Durant with the second pick in 2007 and Gary Payton with the second pick in 1990, they have never had the first overall pick. The Thunder have been recognized for their smart Draft picks, such as Durant, Russell Westbrook, and James Harden, which formed the core of a contending team.

6. Utah Jazz: Founded in 1974 as the New Orleans Jazz before relocating to Salt Lake City in 1979, they have never had the first overall pick in the Draft. Despite this, they have managed to build successful teams, notably with the selections of Karl Malone (13th pick in 1985) and John Stockton (16th pick in 1984), who led the team to two NBA Finals in the 1990s.

The absence of a first overall pick for these teams has not prevented several of them from enjoying considerable success in the league.

Although not having the first pick may seem like a disadvantage, these teams have shown that it is possible to build contending teams through smart selections, talent development, and strategic moves in free agency and the trade market.

The Draft lottery, introduced in 1985 to prevent teams from intentionally losing (tanking) for better Draft positions, has been a key factor in the fortunes of franchises.

However, as the history of these six teams demonstrates, success in the NBA does not solely depend on Draft position but on the ability to identify talent and build a cohesive team.

15

In the 1995 NBA Finals, two of the greatest centers of all time faced off: Hakeem Olajuwon and Shaquille O'Neal.

Hakeem Olajuwon, known for his technical skill, precise moves, and relentless defense, led the Houston Rockets.

On the other hand, Shaquille O'Neal, then in his third year in the NBA and playing for the Orlando Magic, had already begun to showcase his physical dominance in the league.

The Finals were seen as an iconic showdown between two basketball titans.

Olajuwon's Rockets swept the Magic in four games, securing their second consecutive championship.

Olajuwon was spectacular throughout the series, averaging 32.8 points per game and outplaying O'Neal, who, despite a strong performance, could not prevent his team's defeat.

For Shaq, the experience was bitter, as he faced one of the few players who could surpass him in both skill and experience.

After the Finals, a frustrated Shaquille O'Neal decided to challenge Hakeem Olajuwon to a one-on-one duel.

Shaq sent a letter to Olajuwon, suggesting they play a one-on-one game, without the help of their teammates, to see who was truly the best.

The idea captured the attention of the media and fans, generating great anticipation.

The event, dubbed "The War on the Floor," was set to be a televised showdown in a pay-per-view format, which would have made it a unique spectacle in NBA history.

The idea of a one-on-one duel between Shaq and Olajuwon had all the ingredients to be a historic event.

Both players were at the peak of their careers, and the contrast in their playing styles promised a fascinating matchup.

O'Neal, with his brute strength and physical dominance, against Olajuwon, with his elegance, unmatched footwork, and his famous "Dream Shake."

However, despite the excitement and public interest, the duel never took place.

Various factors contributed to the cancellation of the event, including concerns about injuries, contractual issues, and the possibility that the event might not live up to expectations, both from a sporting and commercial perspective.

As a result, what could have been one of the most epic showdowns in NBA history remained in the realm of "what could have been."

The potential Shaq vs. Hakeem showdown remains one of the great "what ifs" in NBA history.

Although it never materialized, the idea of seeing two of the greatest centers of all time face off one-on-one continues to fascinate fans.

The 1995 Finals remain the only direct showdown between the two in a high-pressure setting, with Hakeem Olajuwon emerging victorious, while Shaquille O'Neal had to wait until 2000 to win his first NBA championship with the Los Angeles Lakers.

In retrospect, the cancellation of the event may have been a relief for both players.

A one-on-one duel, though entertaining, might not have fully reflected their skills and accomplishments in a team context, where both thrived and became legends.

16

Derrick Rose, the youngest MVP

Derrick Rose made NBA history in 2011 by becoming the youngest player ever to win the league's Most Valuable Player (MVP) award.

At just 22 years old, Rose, who played for the Chicago Bulls, led his team to a 62-20 regular-season record, the best in the league that year.

Rose averaged 25 points, 7.7 assists, and 4.1 rebounds per game, displaying a level of maturity and skill that surprised many.

His combination of speed, agility, and ball control made him an unstoppable force on the court.

However, Rose's career was hampered by multiple severe injuries, particularly to his knees, preventing him from reaching his full potential in the long run.

Despite these setbacks, his achievement as the youngest MVP remains a highlight in NBA history.

Stephen Curry, the only unanimous MVP

Stephen Curry made history during the 2015-2016 season by becoming the only player in NBA history to be unanimously named MVP.

That season, Curry led the Golden State Warriors to a 73-9 record, the best regular-season record of all time.

He averaged 30.1 points, 6.7 assists, and 5.4 rebounds per game, while setting a record with 402 three-pointers in a single season.

Curry redefined the game with his ability to shoot from long range, changing the way basketball is played.

He received all 121 possible votes for MVP, an unprecedented achievement that highlights his dominance and the impact he had on the league during that season.

Bill Russell, the greatest champion of all

Bill Russell is synonymous with success in the NBA.

With 11 championships won with the Boston Celtics between 1957 and 1969, Russell has more titles than any other player in league history.

Known for his relentless defense, rebounding, and on-court leadership, Russell was a key figure in the Celtics' dynasty during the 1950s and 60s.

His impact goes beyond statistics; Russell was a pioneer in basketball defense and a leader in the civil rights movement off the court.

In honor of his legacy, the NBA named the Finals MVP trophy the "Bill Russell NBA Finals Most Valuable Player Award."

Russell's influence on the game and his unprecedented success make him one of the most important figures in sports history.

17

Larry O'Brien was a key figure in the transformation of the NBA during his tenure as the league's commissioner from 1975 to 1984.

His influence and vision helped shape the NBA into what it is today—one of the most successful and globally recognized sports leagues.

In honor of his legacy, since 1984, the trophy awarded to the NBA champion team bears his name: the Larry O'Brien Trophy.

One of Larry O'Brien's most significant achievements was the merger of the American Basketball Association (ABA) with the NBA in 1976.

This merger was a pivotal moment in the history of professional basketball in the United States, as it solidified the NBA as the country's premier basketball league.

The incorporation of four ABA teams into the NBA (Denver Nuggets, Indiana Pacers, San Antonio Spurs, and New York Nets) not only brought geographic expansion but also an influx of talent, dynamic style of play, and the introduction of elements like the three-point shot, which had been popularized in the ABA.

Another of O'Brien's notable achievements was the implementation of the salary cap in the NBA, a measure aimed at creating greater parity between teams and controlling rising salary costs.

The salary cap allowed the league to avoid extreme disparity between rich and poor teams, promoting greater competitiveness and financial stability.

This policy helped balance the league and prevent teams with the most financial resources from consistently dominating.

Moreover, Larry O'Brien was instrumental in negotiating television deals that elevated the NBA to new heights in terms of popularity and reach.

Under his leadership, the NBA secured the most lucrative television contracts to date, allowing professional basketball to reach a much broader audience and increasing its visibility both in the United States and around the world.

These television deals not only boosted the league's revenue but also cemented the NBA as a premier sports spectacle.

The Larry O'Brien Trophy, awarded to the NBA champion each year, is a symbol of excellence and the pursuit of greatness in basketball.

This trophy is a recognition of O'Brien's legacy and his lasting impact on the league. Made of sterling silver and coated in gold, the trophy stands approximately 61 centimeters tall and weighs 14.5 pounds, representing a basketball over a hoop.

Larry O'Brien's era as commissioner marked a period of fundamental changes in the NBA, establishing many of the structures and policies that have allowed the league to grow exponentially in the following decades.

His leadership not only addressed immediate challenges but also laid the foundation for a prosperous future, ensuring that the NBA could become a global sports powerhouse.

18

Superstitions of NBA players

1. Michael Jordan: Considered by many as the greatest basketball player of all time, he had a well-known superstition: he wore his University of North Carolina shorts under his Chicago Bulls uniform in every game. Jordan believed that the shorts brought him good luck, as he wore them when he won the NCAA championship in 1982. To maintain this tradition, Jordan started wearing longer shorts in the NBA to fit the UNC shorts underneath.

2. LeBron James: He is known for his meticulous pre-game ritual. One of his most iconic superstitions is throwing chalk powder into the air before the start of the game. This ritual has become a trademark part of his routine, and fans often imitate it in the stands. Additionally, LeBron has a specific routine for listening to music and relaxing before games, which he follows to the letter.

3. Shaquille O'Neal: He had several superstitions throughout his career, but one of the strangest involved touching the basket posts before each game. He believed this would help him perform better. Moreover, O'Neal always had a specific pre-game routine that included listening to music and reciting positive affirmations.

4. Jason Kidd: He had an unusual superstition that involved blowing a kiss to the rim every time he shot a free throw. This habit was a gesture toward his wife at the time, but it also became a ritual that helped him focus and stay calm at the free-throw line.

5. Kevin Garnett: Known for his intensity on the court, he had a peculiar superstition: he would hit his head against the basket support before every game.

This ritual was a way to focus and get into "beast mode" before each game. Garnett also had the habit of talking to the rim before taking a free throw, telling it to let the ball go in.

6. Karl Malone: Nicknamed "The Mailman," he had a superstition involving chewing gum during every game. He believed that chewing gum helped him stay relaxed and focused. Additionally, Malone always said a prayer before each game, asking for protection and success in the game.

7. Ray Allen: He had a very precise routine before every game. He would arrive at the stadium hours before the start of the game to practice his shot in complete silence and solitude. This ritual was a way to mentally prepare and achieve an absolute state of concentration before the game began.

8. Paul Pierce: Known as "The Truth," he had a superstition involving the same warm-up routine before every game. This routine included specific stretches and a series of shots from different spots on the court. Pierce also used to eat the same type of food before every game, believing it brought him good luck.

9. Gilbert Arenas: Nicknamed "Agent Zero," he had a superstition related to the number of shots he took during warm-up. Arenas believed he had to take an exact number of shots before feeling ready for the game. If he missed any of his practice shots, he would start over until he reached the number he considered "perfect."

19

Famous quotes from legendary players

1. Michael Jordan:

"I've missed more than 9,000 shots in my career. I've lost almost 300 games. 26 times, I've been trusted to take the game-winning shot and missed. I've failed over and over and over again in my life. And that is why I succeed."

This is a reminder that success is not achieved without facing failures.

2. Kobe Bryant:

"People don't understand how much it takes to get to where I am today. My passion for basketball comes from knowing every detail about the game."

Kobe, known for his "Mamba Mentality," always emphasized the importance of hard work, dedication, and an obsessive focus on perfecting his craft.

3. LeBron James:

"It doesn't matter how many times you fall; what's important is how many times you get up and keep moving forward."

LeBron, one of the most complete players in history, highlights the importance of perseverance and the ability to bounce back from challenges.

4. Magic Johnson:

"I can accept failure; everyone fails at something. But I can't accept not trying."

Magic Johnson, one of the NBA's most charismatic figures, always emphasized the importance of giving your best effort without fear of failure.

5. Larry Bird:

"Pressure is something you feel only when you don't know what you're doing."

Larry Bird, known for his confidence and competitiveness, didn't let pressure affect him, trusting in his preparation and skills.

6. Shaquille O'Neal:

"Excellence is not an act, but a habit. What you do repeatedly is what you become."

Shaq, one of the most dominant centers in history, always stressed the importance of consistency in the pursuit of excellence.

7. Tim Duncan:

"Good, better, best. Never rest until your good is better and your better is best."

Known as "The Big Fundamental," Duncan always focused on constant improvement and perfecting the basics of the game.

8. Allen Iverson:

"We're talking about practice, man. Not a game, not a game, not a game. We're talking about practice."

This reflects Iverson's frustration with the criticism he received during his career and the importance he placed on the actual game over practice.

9. Charles Barkley:

"I'm not a role model. Just because I can dunk a basketball doesn't mean I should raise your kids."

Barkley, known for his bluntness, challenged the notion that athletes should be role models simply because of their status, emphasizing personal responsibility.

10. Bill Russell:

"Basketball is not about being on the court. It's about what you do before you get on the court."

Russell, the greatest champion in NBA history with 11 titles, always emphasized the importance of preparation, teamwork, and mental focus.

11. Hakeem Olajuwon:

"I've learned that success is measured not so much by the position one has reached in life as by the obstacles one has overcome while trying to succeed."

Olajuwon, known for his "Dream Shake" and dominance on both ends of the court, highlights the importance of perseverance and overcoming challenges.

12. Dirk Nowitzki:

"I'm not the fastest, I'm not the strongest, but I'm prepared to win. That's all that matters."

Nowitzki, who revolutionized the power forward position with his shooting ability, underscores the importance of preparation and determination.

20

Countries with the most NBA fans

1. United States: As the home of the NBA, it's no surprise that the U.S. has the largest number of fans. The NBA is an integral part of American sports culture, with millions of people following the league through television, in arenas, and on digital platforms. According to various surveys, around 26 million people in the U.S. consider themselves regular NBA fans, with audiences reaching over 20 million during the Finals.

2. China: China is the second-largest market for the NBA and possibly the country with the most fans outside the United States. Interest in the NBA skyrocketed in China with Yao Ming's entry into the league in 2002, and since then, basketball has become one of the most popular sports in the country. The NBA estimates that over 300 million people in China play basketball, and millions follow the league through platforms like Tencent, which broadcasts games live. During the NBA Finals, viewership in China can reach hundreds of millions.

3. Philippines: The Philippines is one of the most passionate basketball countries in the world. The NBA has a massive following in the country, where basketball is the number one sport. The game is accessible through television broadcasts and online platforms, and the league regularly organizes events and clinics in the country. It is estimated that around 62% of the Filipino population follows the NBA, equating to more than 65 million fans.

4. Canada: The popularity of the NBA in Canada has seen a significant rise, especially after the success of the Toronto Raptors, who won their first championship in 2019.

Canada has the largest number of international players in the NBA, which has increased interest in the league. It is estimated that around 15 million Canadians are NBA followers, with television viewership regularly surpassing millions during the Finals.

5. Brazil: Brazil is one of the most important emerging markets for the NBA in Latin America. Basketball has gained popularity in the country, partly thanks to Brazilian players like Anderson Varejão, Leandro Barbosa, and Tiago Splitter, who have played in the league. It is estimated that Brazil has around 10 million NBA fans, with a steadily growing audience thanks to increased broadcasting of games on cable television and digital platforms.

6. India: India represents a vast and growing market for the NBA. Although cricket remains the dominant sport, the NBA has made significant efforts to promote basketball in India, with initiatives like the NBA Academy and broadcasting games in Hindi. It is estimated that there are over 30 million NBA followers in India, and this number is constantly increasing as the league expands its presence in the country.

7. Mexico: Mexico has a long history with the NBA, and interest in the league has grown significantly in recent years. The proximity to the United States and the broadcasting of games in Spanish have helped increase the popularity of basketball in the country. It is estimated that there are around 20 million NBA fans in Mexico, with events like regular-season games in Mexico City helping to solidify the fan base.

8. Spain: Spain is one of the European countries with a great passion for basketball, thanks in part to the success of Spanish players like Pau Gasol, Marc Gasol, and Ricky Rubio in the NBA.

The country has a strong national league, but the NBA remains very popular, with a significant following on television and social media. It is estimated that around 10 million people in Spain follow the NBA.

9. Australia: Australia has emerged as a country with a growing NBA fan base, driven by the success of Australian players like Andrew Bogut, Ben Simmons, and Patty Mills. Basketball is one of the most popular sports in Australia, and the NBA has gained significant traction in the country. It is estimated that around 6 million people in Australia regularly follow the NBA.

10. Argentina: Argentina has a strong basketball tradition, partly thanks to the "Golden Generation" that won Olympic gold in 2004. The NBA is very popular in the country, especially since players like Manu Ginóbili, Andrés Nocioni, and Luis Scola had successful careers in the league. It is estimated that around 5 million people in Argentina are NBA fans.

21

Tragic deaths and serious accidents of players, both on and off the court

1. Reggie Lewis: A star for the Boston Celtics, Reggie Lewis passed away on July 27, 1993, at the age of 27 after collapsing during a practice at Brandeis University. Lewis had previously collapsed during a playoff game in April of that year against the Charlotte Hornets, but doctors initially thought it was a minor issue. However, after several tests, he was diagnosed with a heart disorder. Despite this, Lewis continued to train. During an informal practice, he collapsed again and could not be revived. His death was due to cardiac arrest, and it was later discovered that he had hypertrophic cardiomyopathy, a condition that thickens the heart muscle.

2. Hank Gathers: Although he was not an NBA player at the time, Hank Gathers is one of the most tragic cases in basketball history. Gathers, who played for Loyola Marymount University, collapsed and died on the court on March 4, 1990, during a West Coast Conference tournament game. He was 23 years old. Gathers had been diagnosed with a heart arrhythmia a few months earlier and was on medication, although it is believed that he was not taking the recommended dosage because it affected his performance. His death shocked the sports world and led to greater attention on athletes' heart health.

3. Len Bias: Although it did not happen on the court, Len Bias's death remains one of the most shocking tragedies in basketball history. Bias, a superstar from the University of Maryland, was selected as the second overall pick in the 1986 NBA Draft by the Boston Celtics. However, just two days after being selected, Bias died from a cocaine overdose in his university dorm room.

His death shook the NBA and had a profound impact on the perception of drug abuse in sports.

4. Dražen Petrović: The Croatian star and New Jersey Nets player died in a car accident on June 7, 1993, at the age of 28. Petrović was traveling in Germany when the car he was in crashed into a truck. His death shocked the international basketball community, as Petrović was considered one of the best European players of his time and was at the peak of his NBA career.

5. Malik Sealy: A player for the Minnesota Timberwolves, Sealy died in a car accident on May 20, 2000. Sealy, 30 years old, was driving home after attending his teammate Kevin Garnett's birthday party when a drunk driver collided head-on with his vehicle. Sealy died instantly. His tragic death deeply affected the Timberwolves, especially Garnett, who was a close friend of Sealy.

6. Bison Dele (Brian Williams): A player who played for several NBA teams and won a championship with the Chicago Bulls in 1997, disappeared in the Pacific Ocean in July 2002 under mysterious circumstances. It is believed that Dele was murdered along with his girlfriend and the captain of his boat by his brother, who later committed suicide. Although this event did not occur on the court, Dele's death remains one of the darkest and most puzzling cases in NBA history.

7. Lorenzen Wright: A former NBA player, Wright was murdered in July 2010. His body was found in a field in Memphis with multiple gunshot wounds. The investigation revealed that he was the victim of a homicide, and years later, his ex-wife was accused of being involved in the crime.

22

Cheating by Professional NBA Players

1. Tim Donaghy and the Referee Scandal: The most infamous case in NBA history doesn't directly involve players but rather a referee. Tim Donaghy, who officiated in the NBA for 13 seasons, was arrested in 2007 for participating in an illegal betting scheme. Donaghy admitted to betting on NBA games, including some he officiated himself, and pleaded guilty to charges of conspiracy to commit fraud and transmitting betting information. He claimed to have influenced officiating decisions to benefit his bets and those of his accomplices. This scandal rocked the NBA and led to a thorough review of referee conduct and league policies to prevent future manipulation.

2. Flopping: Flopping is a tactic used by some players to exaggerate or simulate physical contact with the intent of deceiving referees and drawing favorable fouls. Although technically legal, it is considered a form of cheating that distorts the integrity of the game. Players like LeBron James, Manu Ginóbili, James Harden, and Chris Paul have been accused of flopping on various occasions. The NBA began imposing fines for flopping in 2012 to discourage this behavior, but it remains an issue in the league.

3. Michael Jordan and Gambling: One of the NBA's biggest stars, Michael Jordan, has been surrounded by controversies related to gambling. In 1993, a book by businessman Richard Esquinas alleged that Jordan owed him over a million dollars in golf bets. Although Jordan admitted to enjoying gambling, he denied being addicted. This scandal led to speculation about whether gambling influenced Jordan's brief decision to retire in 1993, though no direct connection has been proven.

4. 1985 Draft Fixing: Although it doesn't involve players, the 1985 NBA Draft has been the subject of conspiracy theories for decades. The NBA introduced the Draft Lottery in 1985, and the New York Knicks won the first pick, selecting Patrick Ewing. Some have suggested that the league rigged the lottery to ensure that Ewing, an emerging star, ended up in a large market like New York. The theory is based on the idea that the envelope containing the Knicks' card was bent or frozen so that NBA Commissioner David Stern could identify it. Although the NBA has categorically denied these accusations, the incident remains a topic of debate among fans.

5. Drug Scandals in the 1970s and 1980s: During the 1970s and 1980s, the NBA faced a significant problem with drug use among its players. Although not cheating in the traditional sense, substance abuse, such as cocaine, affected player performance and the league's reputation. Players like John Drew, Micheal Ray Richardson, and Roy Tarpley were repeatedly suspended for violating the league's drug policy. These issues led the NBA to implement a stricter anti-drug program and to promote a healthier image in the following era.

6. Cheating on Drug Tests: Some players have attempted to cheat on drug tests by using substances or methods to avoid a positive result. These attempts have led to suspensions and fines. A notable example is the 25-game suspension given to Deandre Ayton of the Phoenix Suns in 2019 for using a diuretic, which is a banned substance because it can mask the presence of other drugs in the system.

7. Unsportsmanlike Tactics: Over the years, there have been several tactics considered unsportsmanlike that, while not explicitly breaking the rules, are seen as a form of cheating.

An example is the "Hack-a-Shaq" strategy, which involves intentionally fouling a poor free-throw shooter like Shaquille O'Neal to force free throws and prevent easy points. This tactic has been criticized for distorting the game and has led the NBA to modify its rules to limit its use.

8. Connie Hawkins and the Betting Scandal: A college basketball star who later became an NBA player, Connie Hawkins was implicated in a betting scandal in the late 1950s. Although his direct involvement in game-fixing was never proven, he was expelled from the NCAA and banned from the NBA for several years. Hawkins was eventually exonerated and went on to have a successful career in the NBA.

9. The Cases of Ben Simmons and James Harden:
In recent seasons, players Ben Simmons and James Harden have been involved in controversies regarding their behavior in forcing trades. Harden was accused of not playing to his full potential to pressure the Houston Rockets into trading him to the Brooklyn Nets, while Simmons was accused of faking mental health issues to avoid playing for the Philadelphia 76ers until he was traded. While not cheating in the traditional sense, these incidents raised questions about the professional ethics and sportsmanship of the players involved.

10. The "Frozen Envelopes" Scandal in the 1985 Draft:
One of the most persistent conspiracy theories in NBA history involves the 1985 Draft, where the New York Knicks secured the first pick and selected Patrick Ewing. The theory suggests that Commissioner David Stern manipulated the lottery by freezing or bending the envelope containing the Knicks' name, ensuring that the New York franchise, in a key market, would get the first pick. Although nothing has ever been proven and the league denies any manipulation, this incident remains a recurring topic of discussion.

11. Tanking (Losing on Purpose): Tanking is a strategy where teams intentionally lose games to secure a better position in the NBA Draft. Although not cheating in the traditional sense, it is seen as distorting the competitive spirit. Teams like the Philadelphia 76ers have been accused of tanking, especially during their "The Process" period, where they accumulated numerous losses to secure high draft picks. The NBA has implemented changes in the lottery system to discourage this practice, reducing the odds of the worst teams getting the first pick.

12. Los Angeles Lakers and the Chris Paul Trade: In 2011, the NBA, which at the time controlled the New Orleans Hornets (due to a lack of an owner), vetoed a trade that would have sent Chris Paul to the Los Angeles Lakers. Although not a case of cheating or game-fixing, the fact that the league blocked a move favorable to one of its most important franchises generated significant controversy and speculation about a possible conflict of interest. Some critics argued that the NBA was manipulating competitive balance to prevent the Lakers from becoming even more dominant.

13. Injury Manipulation Cases: There have been suspicions that teams and players have exaggerated or downplayed the severity of injuries to gain a competitive advantage. A famous example is the speculation surrounding Kawhi Leonard's injury during his time with the San Antonio Spurs. While Leonard and his medical team claimed his injury was severe, some within the Spurs organization believed Leonard could have returned sooner. This disagreement contributed to his eventual departure from the team.

23

Julius Randle

Born on November 29, 1994, in Dallas, Texas, Julius Randle is a professional basketball player who has had a successful NBA career since his debut in 2014.

Standing at 2.06 meters (6 feet 9 inches) tall and weighing around 113 kg, Randle primarily plays as a power forward.

His career has been marked by ups and downs, but he has always been recognized for his work ethic and potential.

Randle grew up in an environment heavily influenced by basketball. His mother, Carolyn Kyles, played college basketball, and his godfather, Jeff Webster, was a standout player at the University of Oklahoma and had a brief NBA career with the Washington Bullets.

This family background provided him with a strong foundation and an early love for the sport, allowing him to develop his skills from a young age.

During his high school years at Prestonwood Christian Academy in Plano, Texas, Randle stood out as one of the best players of his generation. He was widely regarded as one of the top recruits in the nation, and his statistics supported that reputation.

In his senior year of high school, he averaged an impressive 32.5 points and 22.5 rebounds per game, which catapulted him into the national spotlight.

His dominance on the court earned him multiple honors, including being named a McDonald's All-American.

After an intense recruiting process, Julius Randle chose to play for the University of Kentucky, one of the most prestigious college basketball programs in the United States.

Under the guidance of coach John Calipari, Randle had an outstanding college season.

He averaged 15 points and 10.4 rebounds per game, leading the Kentucky Wildcats to the NCAA tournament final in 2014.

Although Kentucky lost to the University of Connecticut, Randle was named to the NCAA All-Tournament Team and solidified his place as one of the top prospects for the NBA Draft.

In the 2014 NBA Draft, Randle was selected seventh overall by the Los Angeles Lakers.

For a young man who grew up admiring players like Kobe Bryant and LeBron James, being drafted by the Lakers was a dream come true, but his NBA career had a challenging start.

In his debut on October 28, 2014, against the Houston Rockets, Randle suffered a fractured tibia in his right leg after scoring his first two points in the league.

The injury forced him to miss the rest of the 2014-2015 season, which was a tough blow for both him and the Lakers.

Despite the severity of his injury, Randle worked tirelessly to recover.

He documented his rehabilitation process through videos on social media, showcasing his dedication and discipline.

The Lakers, for their part, remained optimistic about his future, confident in his ability to overcome this obstacle.

In the 2015-2016 season, Randle returned to action, playing in 81 games and averaging 11.3 points and 10.2 rebounds per game, proving that he was ready to make his mark in the league.

Over time, Randle continued to improve and diversify his game.

After four seasons with the Lakers, he joined the New Orleans Pelicans in 2018, where he had a breakout season, averaging 21.4 points and 8.7 rebounds per game.

In 2019, he signed with the New York Knicks, where he finally established himself as a star.

In the 2020-2021 season, Randle had an exceptional performance, averaging 24.1 points, 10.2 rebounds, and 6 assists per game, earning his first All-Star selection and the NBA's Most Improved Player award.

Julius Randle is known for his versatility and ability to play both inside and outside the paint.

His combination of strength, agility, and ball-handling skills makes him difficult to defend.

Additionally, he has significantly improved his mid-range and long-distance shooting, making him a more complete threat on the court.

His ability to distribute the ball has also improved, allowing him to be a playmaker from the power forward position.

24

Steve Nash

Steve Nash is a former basketball player who left an indelible mark on the NBA during his 19 seasons in the league, playing for four different teams.

He was born on February 7, 1974, in Johannesburg, South Africa, but was raised in Canada.

Nash moved to the United States on a basketball scholarship to attend Santa Clara University, as there were limited opportunities to develop his talent in this sport in Canada.

Steve Nash's arrival in the NBA in 1996 was somewhat bittersweet.

Although it was a dream come true for him, he was not well received by fans and some critics, who considered his selection in the Draft to be unfair because he was not a well-known name in the American college basketball scene.

However, Nash soon proved his worth with his unique playing style, focusing on his ability to distribute assists and his shooting accuracy, which would make him one of the best point guards in NBA history.

Throughout his career, Nash played for teams such as the Phoenix Suns, Dallas Mavericks, and Los Angeles Lakers, but it was with the Suns where he made his most significant impact.

In his second stint with the Phoenix Suns, starting in 2004, Nash reached the peak of his career, averaging 110.4 points per game in the 2004-2005 season.

This impressive achievement made him the first Canadian to win the NBA Most Valuable Player (MVP) award, a title he repeated in 2006.

Nash revolutionized the game with his court vision and his ability to lead the offense, becoming one of the leaders of the fast-paced, high-scoring style that defined the Suns during those years.

Interestingly, Steve Nash was nicknamed "Almodóvar Nash" in Spain due to his admiration for Spanish film director Pedro Almodóvar, something he has proudly acknowledged.

This nickname reflects not only his connection to Spanish culture but also his global influence as a player.

In addition to his basketball career, Nash is known for his skill in other sports.

He is an excellent soccer and hockey player, sports he practices in his free time.

This multi-sport talent highlights his exceptional athletic ability.

Nash also stood out off the court by earning a degree in Sociology from Santa Clara University, demonstrating that he is as accomplished in academics as he is in sports.

Nash also made history by becoming the first Canadian to play in an All-Star Game in 2002, solidifying his place as a pioneer of Canadian basketball.

His legacy is measured not only in terms of awards and statistics but also in how he redefined the role of the point guard in modern NBA.

25
Paul George

Paul George is one of the most prominent players in the NBA, best known for his time with the Indiana Pacers, although his career has continued successfully with other teams in the league.

Born on May 2, 1990, in Palmdale, California, George stands 2.06 meters tall and has played as a shooting guard and small forward, excelling in versatility, defensive skills, and scoring ability.

Throughout his career, he has been the subject of speculation and debate about whether he is a rising superstar, and his personal achievements suggest that he certainly is.

One of the most notorious incidents in Paul George's career occurred during a game between the Indiana Pacers and the Chicago Bulls, where he was fined $15,000 and ejected from the game for kicking a ball that accidentally hit an assistant in the face.

George explained that he did not intend to hit anyone and that his goal was to kick the ball against a wooden bar that separates the court from the stands.

After the incident, he publicly apologized to the affected woman, demonstrating his character and responsibility despite the unfortunate event.

Another interesting fact about Paul George is his family connection to basketball.

His older sister, Telosha George, also played basketball during her college years at Pepperdine University in Malibu.

Although she never made it to the Women's Professional Basketball League, Telosha shared a passion for the sport with her brother, highlighting the influence of basketball in the George family.

Paul George's personal life hasn't been without controversy. One of the most talked-about scandals in his career involved rumors that he had impregnated a stripper from Miami and was allegedly willing to pay her a million dollars to have an abortion.

This rumor surfaced at the same time it was reported that George's then-girlfriend, Callie Rivers, was also pregnant.

According to reports, the stripper, named Daniela, rejected George's alleged offer and decided to have the baby.

Although George never confirmed these rumors, the scandal was a hot topic in the media and among fans.

Another significant moment in Paul George's life was when he suffered a severe injury during a practice game for the Basketball World Cup, where George broke his tibia and fibula, sidelining him for nearly a year.

This injury was a devastating blow to his career, and the basketball community rallied in support, making the hashtag #PrayForPaulGeorge a trending topic on Twitter.

However, George found a unique way to lift his spirits during his recovery: he bought a Ferrari 458, which he shared on his Instagram account.

Although he couldn't drive it due to his injury, purchasing the car was a symbolic way of staying positive and motivated.

26

Nicolas Batum

Nicolas Batum is a French basketball player who has had a notable career both in the NBA and on the international stage.

Born on December 14, 1988, in Lisieux, France, Batum is considered one of the most talented players his country has produced.

He currently plays as a small forward for the Charlotte Hornets in the NBA, wearing the number 5.

Although he hasn't played in an NBA Finals, Batum has achieved several titles and medals with the French national team in international competitions, making him an important figure in European basketball.

One of the most remarkable facts about Nicolas Batum is that he became a father for the first time in 2016, just before a crucial playoff game.

The birth of his son occurred hours before Game 6 of the playoff series between the Charlotte Hornets and the Miami Heat.

This personal event affected his performance in the game, as he appeared tired due to a lack of sleep.

Despite his exhaustion, Batum played in the game, and afterward, he was greeted by his teammates in the locker room with balloons and congratulations to celebrate the arrival of his son.

This moment highlights the importance of family to Batum and how he managed to balance his personal and professional life at a crucial point in his career.

Another significant anecdote in Batum's career occurred during the 2012 London Olympics, where he represented France.

In a highly contested game against Spain, Batum was involved in a controversial incident when, with 24 seconds remaining and France trailing, he punched Spanish player Juan Carlos Navarro in the stomach.

This act of frustration provoked the anger of the Spanish players, who quickly confronted Batum about his behavior.

The incident caused a major stir in the sports world and became one of the most controversial moments in Batum's career.

A year after the Olympic incident, Batum again generated controversy when he placed a sign in the locker room of the Portland Trail Blazers, the team he was playing for at the time, that read: "We will not lose to Spanish players."

This gesture was interpreted by many as an offense towards Spanish players, given the rivalry between the two countries in basketball.

However, Batum explained that his intention was not to insult the Spanish players but to motivate himself and his team.

He later apologized and clarified that he had deep respect for his Spanish opponents.

Throughout his career, Nicolas Batum has been respected for his on-court skills, combining technique and physicality to become a versatile and effective small forward.

27

Joe Johnson

Born on June 29, 1981, in Little Rock, Arkansas,
Joe Johnson is a veteran NBA player who has made
a significant impact throughout his long career.

With over ten seasons in the league, Johnson has been
known for his scoring ability, reliability in clutch moments,
and longevity in professional basketball.

Here are some of the most notable facts about Joe Johnson,
a player who has managed to stay relevant in the league for
nearly two decades.

Joe Johnson has participated in an impressive 11
postseasons over his 17 seasons in the NBA,
but he has never won a championship ring.

During his time with the Atlanta Hawks, Johnson
was a key player, leading them to five consecutive
postseasons between 2008 and 2013.

In that period, he reached three conference finals,
showcasing his ability to take his team to the highest
level, although he never made it to the NBA Finals.

Later, with the Brooklyn Nets, Johnson experienced
similar success, qualifying for the playoffs three
consecutive times between 2012 and 2015.

In 2014, the Nets reached the conference semifinals,
but once again, Johnson fell short in his pursuit of a title.

His time with the Miami Heat also led him to a conference
semifinal, but once again, his team was eliminated.

Despite his consistency in leading his teams to the playoffs, Johnson has never had the opportunity to compete in an NBA Finals.

Throughout his career, Joe Johnson has played for five different NBA teams.

He began his career with the Boston Celtics in 2001 but was traded to the Phoenix Suns during his rookie season, where he played until 2005.

He then joined the Atlanta Hawks, where he enjoyed his most prolific period, playing there from 2005 to 2012.

He later played for the Brooklyn Nets from 2012 to 2016, before briefly joining the Miami Heat.

This experience with multiple teams allowed Johnson to adapt to different playing styles and roles, showcasing his versatility and ability to contribute in various situations.

One of the most notable aspects of Joe Johnson's game is his ability as a three-point shooter.

Throughout his career, he established himself as one of the best three-point shooters in NBA history, ranking eleventh on the list of players with the most three-pointers made.

His accuracy from long range made him a constant threat to opposing defenses, and his ability to score in crucial moments earned him the nickname "Iso Joe" for his skill in generating points in one-on-one situations.

In 2016, when Johnson was considering his options at the end of his career, he had the opportunity to join LeBron James' Cleveland Cavaliers, which many believed would give him a great chance to win a championship ring.

However, Johnson chose to sign with the Miami Heat, a decision that surprised many.

He preferred to stay in South Beach, partly for personal reasons, such as his desire to avoid the cold weather in the northern United States and his close friendship with Pat Riley, one of the Heat's executives.

Additionally, his decision reflected his desire to think about his family and find an environment where he felt comfortable ending his career.

Joe Johnson is also known for having a large family, and on one occasion, he brought so many relatives to a game that they filled an entire section of the stadium.

This was so impressive that a commentator joked that Johnson's family was larger than the population of Grenada.

This comment reflects the support Johnson has received from his family throughout his career, a crucial aspect of his success and longevity in the NBA.

Joe Johnson's path to the NBA was not easy, but his parents always believed in his potential, and despite financial difficulties, they made significant sacrifices to pay for his training and basketball academies.

These efforts paid off when Johnson was selected in the NBA Draft and began a career that, although filled with ups and downs, has been impressive in terms of individual achievements and longevity.

28

DeMar DeRozan

DeMar DeRozan is a prominent American professional basketball player, best known for his time with the Toronto Raptors in the NBA, although he currently plays for the Chicago Bulls.

Born on August 7, 1989, in Compton, California, DeRozan has established himself as one of the most talented shooting guards in the league, recognized for his scoring ability and offensive prowess.

Throughout his career, he has represented the United States in international competitions, winning gold medals at the 2016 Rio de Janeiro Olympics and the 2014 Basketball World Cup.

While he is well-known for his on-court achievements, DeRozan also has several stories and interesting facts that reveal more personal and lesser-known aspects of his life and career.

One of the most notable facts about DeMar DeRozan's career is his record with the Toronto Raptors.

During his time with the team, he became the player with the most games played in the franchise's history.

He reached this milestone at the age of 27 years and 124 days, surpassing the previous record set by Morris Peterson, who played 542 games with the Raptors over a seven-year period.

By September 2016, DeRozan had played 543 games with the Canadian team, solidifying his place as one of the most important figures in the franchise's history.

Another curious and somewhat embarrassing incident in DeRozan's career occurred during an interview with ESPN's Doris Burke at the Air Canada Centre.

Despite being a star of the team, DeRozan was stopped by a security guard who did not recognize him and asked for his identification.

Even though DeRozan tried to explain that he was a member of the Raptors and was there for an interview, the guard did not believe him until another security staff member recognized him and cleared up the situation.

Although the misunderstanding was quickly resolved, DeRozan later confessed that the incident made him feel like his ego had been "demolished" by not being recognized in his own arena, a place where he had shined on numerous occasions.

Beyond his professional life, DeMar DeRozan is known for his deep dedication to his family, especially to his mother.

DeRozan has stated in several interviews that his main motivation for playing basketball is not fame or wealth but the ability to provide a better quality of life for his mother, who suffers from lupus, a chronic disease that requires expensive and constant medical treatments.

DeRozan has done everything possible to ensure that his mother receives the best care possible, and his success on the court has allowed him to afford those treatments.

His $145 million contract, signed with the Raptors in 2016, has been largely dedicated to ensuring the well-being of his mother and his family, demonstrating his commitment and love for them.

29
Ray Allen

Ray Allen is one of the most iconic figures in basketball history, primarily recognized for his exceptional three-point shooting ability and his significant impact on the NBA.

Throughout his career, Allen was selected for the NBA All-Star Game nine times and solidified his place as the player with the most three-pointers made in basketball history, with a total of 2,973, surpassing the legend Reggie Miller, who ranks second with 2,560 three-pointers.

In addition to his NBA achievements, Ray Allen was also a key player on the United States basketball team that won the gold medal at the 2000 Sydney Olympics, contributing to his country's dominance in the sport.

One of the most interesting facts about Ray Allen is his training routine, as he was known for his meticulous work ethic, which included the habit of warming up before any other player.

It's also worth noting that he would arrive early to practice and shoot on an empty court, allowing him to perfect his shot without distractions.

He also had the peculiar habit of chewing gum while training, something that became part of his routine.

This dedication to training and mental and physical preparation was key to his success and longevity in the NBA.

Ray Allen's childhood was also marked by constant relocations due to his father, Walter Allen, who was in the military.

His family lived on several military bases in the United States, including in Oklahoma and California, and also spent time in European countries such as England and Germany.

This nomadic life gave Ray a unique perspective and resilience, traits that he would later apply in his sports career.

Despite these constant moves, the Allen family settled for a time in South Carolina, where Ray attended high school and began to excel in basketball.

In addition to his basketball career, Ray Allen ventured into acting.

Two years after entering the NBA, while playing for the Milwaukee Bucks, Allen starred in the movie *"He Got Game,"* directed by the renowned filmmaker Spike Lee.

In the film, Allen played the lead character, a young basketball prodigy named Jesus Shuttlesworth.

The movie, which explored the challenges and pressures of being a talented young athlete, also featured performances by Denzel Washington and Milla Jovovich.

Allen's participation in the film showcased him in a different light and demonstrated his ability to stand out off the court.

A curious and alarming incident occurred in 2014 when a group of teenagers, who were fans of Ray Allen, broke into his house during the night.

While Allen and his family were sleeping, the teenagers, who were at a party in the neighborhood, decided to enter his home—not with the intention to steal, but simply to get a closer look at their idol.

However, they were startled and ran away when they realized they had been discovered.

Although they didn't take anything or cause any damage, the incident highlighted the extent of Allen's fame and how it can affect the privacy of celebrities.

The teenagers involved were required to perform community service as a consequence of their actions.

30

Isiah Thomas

Isiah Thomas is one of the most iconic players in NBA history, known for his leadership, skill, and tenacity on the court.

He played for the Detroit Pistons throughout his entire professional career, which began when he was just 20 years old.

From a young age, Thomas demonstrated unwavering passion and commitment to basketball, which led him to become one of the greatest point guards of all time.

From his youth, Isiah Thomas was characterized by his discipline.

During his school years, he would wake up every day at five in the morning to arrive early at school, as his commute took about 90 minutes.

This level of dedication and enthusiasm for his studies and training was an early indication of the work ethic that would define him as a professional player.

Physically, Isiah Thomas had a unique appearance.

Although he stood at 1.85 meters (6'1"), a respectable height for a point guard, his youthful face and build made him appear younger than he actually was.

This appearance led many people to underestimate him, but on the court, Thomas was relentless, and his nickname, "The Baby-faced Assassin," perfectly captured this duality.

Despite his innocent face, Thomas was known for his aggressiveness and competitiveness in the game.

He was nicknamed "The Baby-faced Assassin" by a coach who, when asked why he used that nickname, explained that Thomas "cuts you after he smiles at you."

This nickname reflected his ability to play with fierce intensity while maintaining a friendly appearance.

Isiah Thomas's arrival at the Detroit Pistons marked a significant shift in the team's culture.

Under his leadership, the Pistons transformed into the "Bad Boys," a team known for their physical and tough playing style that intimidated their opponents.

Thomas's aggressiveness and his ability to lead his team in crucial moments contributed to the Pistons becoming one of the most feared teams in the league during the late 1980s and early 1990s.

However, this reputation also generated intense rivalries, the most notable being with Michael Jordan and the Chicago Bulls.

The rivalry between Isiah Thomas and Michael Jordan is legendary.

It intensified especially after the Chicago Bulls swept the Pistons in the 1991 Eastern Conference Finals, winning the series 4-0.

In an act that many interpreted as unsportsmanlike, Thomas and his teammates left the court before the game ended, without congratulating or saying goodbye to the Bulls players.

This incident left a lasting impression on fans and on Jordan, who mentioned Isiah Thomas as one of his greatest motivations to improve in his 2009 Hall of Fame induction speech.

Off the court, Isiah Thomas has also faced challenges.

In 2008, while working as an assistant coach for the New York Knicks, he experienced an incident related to the use of medication.

Thomas took an excessive amount of Lunesta, a sleep medication, which resulted in an overdose.

He was rushed to White Plains Hospital Center in New York but was fortunately discharged the same day.

This incident attracted media attention and raised concerns about his well-being, but Thomas managed to recover quickly.

31

J.R. Smith

Born on September 9, 1985, in Freehold, New Jersey, J.R. Smith is a basketball player known for his talent, passion for the sport, and electrifying style of play.

Introduced to basketball at an early age by his uncle, Smith quickly developed a love for the game that led him to become a professional athlete.

Throughout his career, he has played for several NBA teams, including the New Orleans Hornets, Denver Nuggets, New York Knicks, Cleveland Cavaliers, and Los Angeles Lakers.

While he is known for his successes and accolades, there are several interesting facts about his life and career that reveal unique aspects of his personality and journey.

From his high school days, J.R. Smith showed an unwavering commitment to basketball.

He trained intensely and maintained a clear focus on improving his skills with the goal of reaching the NBA.

This level of dedication reflected his desire to belong to a professional team, and eventually, his hard work paid off when he was selected in the 2004 NBA Draft.

One of the most notable characteristics of J.R. Smith is his love for tattoos.

His body is almost entirely covered with tattoos that represent his beliefs, memories, and tributes to people who have inspired him, including other basketball players like Vince Carter and Michael Jordan.

Smith got his first tattoo at the age of 16 and has continued adding designs to his skin ever since.

Interestingly, when he was younger, he used to criticize people with tattoos, but he later became someone who embodies that very style.

The notoriety of his tattoos was so great that in 2015, the American company Fresh Brewed Tees launched t-shirts that replicated Smith's tattooed upper body.

These shirts were a huge success, selling thousands in a short time, demonstrating the cultural impact Smith has had both on and off the court.

However, J.R. Smith's career hasn't been without challenges, particularly due to his temperament.

Throughout his time in the NBA, his character and discipline issues have been significant obstacles.

During his stint with the New Orleans Hornets, his coach, Byron Scott, was disappointed by Smith's negative attitude and lack of discipline, which eventually led to his departure from the team.

Smith later joined the Denver Nuggets, but his behavioral issues continued.

One of the most notorious incidents occurred during a brawl in a game against the New York Knicks, resulting in a ten-game suspension for Smith.

Despite these challenges, J.R. Smith managed to get his career back on track.

In 2012, he joined the New York Knicks, the same team with which he had the famous altercation.

With the Knicks, Smith experienced a resurgence in his career, achieving significant victories and enhancing his recognition as a professional player.

His talent and ability to score in crucial moments made him a key figure on the team, and in 2013, he won the NBA Sixth Man of the Year award, solidifying his place in the league.

Throughout his career, Smith has also been part of historic moments, such as when he won two NBA championships: one with the Cleveland Cavaliers in 2016, where he was an integral part of the team that came back from a 3-1 deficit in the Finals against the Golden State Warriors, and another with the Los Angeles Lakers in 2020.

32

Sam Cassell

Sam Cassell is a former professional basketball player who has made a significant impact both in the NBA and in coaching.

Born on November 18, 1969, in Baltimore, Maryland, Cassell played in the NBA for 15 seasons and is currently an assistant coach for the Los Angeles Clippers.

Although he is known for his on-court skills and contributions to various teams, there are several interesting facts about Cassell that provide deeper insight into his personality and career.

From a young age, Sam Cassell showed a natural inclination towards sports, particularly basketball.

His passion for the game developed throughout his youth, leading him to stand out as an amateur basketball player in school.

This early dedication to the sport laid the foundation for his future career in the NBA.

Off the court, Cassell is known for his friendliness and extroverted nature.

He is someone who always has a smile on his face and is famous for his good humor and talkative personality.

In fact, his former coach Mike Dunleavy once commented that Cassell talked so much that it was sometimes hard to understand him.

This trait became an integral part of his personality and made him well-liked among his teammates and coaches.

Cuttino Mobley, a former teammate, jokingly said that he had the impression that even Sam didn't understand himself most of the time.

Like many athletes, Cassell had idols he admired who inspired him in his career.

Two figures who influenced his playing style were Terrell Brandon, a former player for the Cleveland Cavaliers, and Jeff Hornacek, known for his time with the Utah Jazz.

These players served as role models for Cassell, guiding his approach and technique on the court.

During his career, Sam Cassell also managed to accumulate significant earnings.

Between the 2007 and 2009 seasons, Cassell earned $7,845,907, a substantial sum that reflects both his talent and his value to the teams he played for.

A curious and distinctive aspect of Cassell is the shape of his head, which has led some to compare him to an "alien."

This nickname, although peculiar, never bothered Cassell.

He took it with good humor and it was never an issue for him, demonstrating his ability to laugh at himself and maintain a positive attitude toward criticism or jokes.

Cassell is also known for being a "nomad" in the NBA, having played for eight different teams over his 15 seasons in the league.

Despite his constant team changes, he never stayed with any of them for more than four years.

This journey allowed him to experience different playing styles and adapt to new dynamics, which ultimately contributed to his success in the league.

Despite his itinerant career, Cassell proved to be an exceptional player, with the ability to make an impact on any team he joined.

His scoring ability, on-court leadership, and knack for making crucial decisions made him a valuable player on every team he played for.

33

James Harden

Born on August 26, 1989, in Los Angeles, California, James Harden is considered one of the best basketball players of the modern NBA era.

Known for his offensive prowess, scoring ability, and unmistakable beard, Harden has left an indelible mark on the world of basketball.

From his high school days to his standout college career at Arizona State University, Harden has accumulated achievements that have propelled him to become an NBA superstar.

One of the most distinctive features of James Harden is his iconic beard.

This physical trait has become his personal trademark and has inspired many fans to imitate him by wearing fake beards at games.

However, what many don't know is that Harden started growing his beard simply out of laziness, as he didn't like shaving.

In an interview, he joked that he would only shave his beard for an offer of ten million dollars.

This look has not only made him easily recognizable but has also generated considerable brand value for him.

Despite being known for his speed, agility, and smooth moves on the court, Harden has had to deal with a significant obstacle: asthma.

From a young age, he has lived with this condition, which has sometimes interfered with his performance on the court.

During his time as an amateur player at Arizona State University, Harden carried an inhaler with him to manage his symptoms during games.

Despite this challenge, it hasn't held him back, and he has managed to excel as one of the most dynamic and difficult players to defend in the NBA.

In the NBA, James Harden has broken numerous records, but one of the most memorable occurred on February 26, 2013, when he was playing for the Houston Rockets.

In a game against his former team, the Oklahoma City Thunder, Harden stood out by scoring 46 points, surpassing his previous record.

This performance further solidified his reputation as one of the most dominant offensive players in the league and demonstrated his ability to elevate his game in crucial moments.

Throughout his career, Harden has also faced difficult moments, such as an incident during his time with the Oklahoma City Thunder.

In a game against the Los Angeles Lakers, Harden was the victim of a violent elbow from Metta World Peace, formerly known as Ron Artest.

The blow caused Harden to suffer a concussion, leading to a seven-game suspension for World Peace.

This incident was a reminder of the intensity and danger that can be present in the NBA, but it also highlighted Harden's resilience, as he recovered and continued to shine in the league.

34

Danny Green

His full name is Daniel Richard Green Jr., and he is an American professional basketball player known for his solid NBA career and his standout participation in college basketball.

Born on June 22, 1987, in North Babylon, New York, Green has been a key figure on several NBA teams, including the San Antonio Spurs, Toronto Raptors, Los Angeles Lakers, and Philadelphia 76ers.

Throughout his career, Green has won multiple NBA championships and is recognized for his three-point shooting and defense.

However, beyond his achievements on the court, there are several interesting facts about Danny Green that reveal unique aspects of his life and personality.

One of the most notable curiosities about Danny Green is his peculiar love for reptiles, specifically snakes.

Unlike most people, Green has a deep interest in these animals and has expressed his love for them on social media.

In fact, he owns two pet snakes: a female named Jade, who is three meters long, and a male named Lightening, who is one meter long.

This unusual interest in reptiles has led to some curious situations, such as one that occurred in 2014 during a game at the AT&T Center against the Portland Trail Blazers.

After the game, several Blazers players started screaming upon discovering a snake in the locker room.

Given Green's well-known love for snakes, some players suspected that he had brought the animal into the locker room as a prank.

However, it was later clarified that the snake had accidentally entered due to a nearby demolition close to the stadium.

The snake, which was non-venomous, was safely removed and returned to its natural habitat.

Another aspect of Danny Green that has garnered attention is his behavior on social media, which has occasionally gotten him into trouble.

One of the most controversial incidents occurred on October 5, 2014, when Green posted a photo of himself at a Holocaust memorial with the hashtag "laugh out loud."

The post was quickly criticized for being insensitive and disrespectful, leading to a barrage of negative comments on social media.

The image was soon deleted, and Green and his communications team issued a public apology.

This incident highlighted the importance of sensitivity on social media and had a negative impact on Green's public image for a time.

35

Yao Ming

Born on September 12, 1980, in Shanghai, China, Yao Ming is one of the most iconic figures in basketball history, known for both his extraordinary height and his impact on the NBA and global basketball.

As an only child due to China's strict birth control policies, Yao was destined for a career in basketball, given that both his father and mother were prominent basketball players in their country.

Throughout his life, Yao has been the subject of many interesting facts and notable achievements that have contributed to his legendary status.

From a young age, Yao Ming stood out for his height.

At 9 years old, he was already significantly taller than most children his age, leading his parents to enroll him in basketball academies.

As he grew, his height continued to increase, eventually reaching 7 feet 6 inches (2.29 meters), making him one of the tallest players in NBA history.

With his arms extended, Yao's reach spanned 3 meters, giving him a significant advantage on the court.

Interestingly, despite his future in basketball, Yao did not like the sport as a child.

It was his mother who took him to a Harlem Globetrotters show, an exhibition team known for their creative ball-handling and entertaining approach to the game.

This event changed Yao's perception of basketball and inspired him to pursue a career in the sport.

At the age of 7, Yao Ming suffered from a kidney problem that resulted in a 70% loss of hearing in his left ear.

This hearing impairment forced him to rely more on visual cues and gestures throughout his life, both on and off the court.

This challenge did not prevent Yao from becoming a successful basketball player and adapting to the needs of the game.

In 2002, Yao Ming was selected by the Houston Rockets as the first overall pick in the NBA draft, becoming the first foreign player to enter the American league without having previously played at a North American university.

Despite his success in the Chinese league, his early years in the NBA were challenging.

His initial averages for points and rebounds were modest, leading some critics, such as NBA legend Charles Barkley, to doubt his ability.

Barkley famously said that Yao wouldn't be able to score more than 20 points in a game and bet that he would kiss a donkey's backside if Yao achieved that feat.

Ironically, Yao scored exactly 20 points in his next game against the Los Angeles Lakers, leading Barkley to fulfill his promise in a scene that remains memorable for many.

Despite his success in the NBA, Yao Ming's career was marred by health issues, particularly related to his knees.

His great height and the physical demands of the NBA began to take a toll on his body.

Starting from his fifth season, Yao suffered several injuries, and ultimately, in 2011, he was forced to retire at the age of 31 due to ongoing knee complications that made it difficult for him to run and jump.

Off the court, Yao Ming is known for his passion for wine.

After retiring, he purchased land and turned it into a vineyard, demonstrating his interest in viticulture and his desire to explore new passions.

Additionally, Yao is passionate about video games, particularly those involving virtual reality, and he has equipped his home in Texas with advanced gaming systems.

Another interesting fact about Yao Ming is his love for speed and car racing.

However, due to his size, he has never been able to drive a single-seater sports car, as he simply doesn't fit in the seats of these cars.

This highlights how his height, which gave him an advantage in basketball, has also been a limitation in other aspects of his life.

36

Julius Erving

Popularly known as "Dr. J," Julius Erving is one of the most iconic and revolutionary players in basketball history.

Born on February 22, 1950, in Roosevelt, New York, Erving stood out from an early age, displaying exceptional talent at the University of Massachusetts, where his spectacular playing style catapulted him to stardom.

Throughout his career, Erving not only left an indelible mark on professional basketball but also became a cultural symbol during the 1970s and early 1980s.

When Julius Erving decided to become a professional player, basketball in the United States was divided between two leagues: the American Basketball Association (ABA) and the National Basketball Association (NBA).

Erving began his career in the ABA, playing for the Virginia Squires and later for the New York Nets.

It was in the ABA where Erving solidified his status as a superstar, standing out for his athletic ability, acrobatic style, and his capacity to execute spectacular "chutes" or "dunks" that had never been seen before.

Erving became a symbol of the ABA, where he won two championships and was named Most Valuable Player (MVP) three times.

During his time in the ABA, he was also known for his distinctive afro hairstyle, which became an integral part of his public image.

Sports commentators of the time even mentioned his height "from the heels to the top of the afro," highlighting the cultural impact of his appearance.

When the ABA dissolved in 1976, Julius Erving joined the NBA as part of the Philadelphia 76ers.

His arrival in the NBA was monumental, as he brought an innovative playing style that mixed athleticism and creativity, deeply influencing the development of modern basketball.

With the 76ers, Erving continued his legacy of excellence, winning a championship in 1983 and being named NBA MVP in 1981.

In total, Erving was selected 16 times for the All-Star Game, both in the ABA and the NBA, and he is one of the few players in history to have scored over 30,000 points in his professional career.

Additionally, his achievements extend to being one of the few players to have won championships in both the ABA and the NBA, underscoring his impact in both leagues.

Despite his success on the court, Julius Erving's personal life was marked by turbulence and controversy.

In 2003, his marriage ended in divorce due to an extramarital affair, and he later remarried.

A particularly notable aspect of his personal life is the relationship with his daughter, tennis player Alexandra Stevenson, born from an extramarital relationship.

Erving never publicly acknowledged Stevenson nor attended her matches, even though she managed to reach the semifinals at Wimbledon.

In 2009, they reunited in a televised interview that proved to be awkward and did little to mend their relationship.

Another interesting fact is that Julius Erving is the only player in NBA history to have his jersey retired by two different teams: the New York Nets (ABA) and the Philadelphia 76ers (NBA).

The Nets retired the number 32 in his honor, while the 76ers retired the number 6, the numbers Erving wore during his time with both teams.

37

Patrick Mills

Commonly known as Patty Mills, he is an Australian basketball player who has made a significant impact both in the NBA and in international basketball.

Born on August 11, 1988, in Canberra, Australia, Mills has been a cornerstone of the San Antonio Spurs, where he has played as a point guard wearing the number 8.

His speed, ability to score from long distance, and leadership have made him a valuable player both for his NBA team and for the Australian national team.

In 2008, Patrick Mills became the youngest Australian player to represent his country in the Olympic Games.

At just 19 years old, he was selected to be part of Australia's basketball team for the Beijing Olympics.

This achievement not only highlighted his talent but also his potential to become a basketball star.

Mills continued to be a key figure in the Australian national team, known as the "Boomers," in international competitions, including the 2012, 2016, and 2020 Olympics.

An interesting anecdote related to Mills is his participation in a famous television commercial in Texas, alongside his San Antonio Spurs teammates.

In the commercial, the Argentine Manu Ginóbili and the Spaniard Pau Gasol prepare a barbecue, a tradition deeply rooted in Argentina and Spain.

In the scene, they invite Danny Green and Patrick Mills to try the feast, speaking to them in Spanish.

Although Mills clarifies in the commercial that he doesn't speak Spanish, his reaction when he tries the grilled ribs is very funny and memorable, showcasing his good humor and ability to adapt to the team's culture.

During the 2016 Rio de Janeiro Olympics, Patrick Mills and his Australian basketball teammates shared several jokes on social media about the conditions in the Olympic Village where they were staying.

They compared the modest facilities to those of the U.S. team, which was staying on a luxurious cruise ship.

In a press conference, Mills joked, "We like to sleep very close to our teammates," referring to the cramped and uncomfortable spaces they were in.

Patty Mills is the first Aboriginal Australian player to reach the NBA, a significant achievement that highlights diversity and inclusion in professional sports.

However, his path was not easy.

During his youth, Mills faced racial prejudice, especially in high school, where he was often discriminated against by his peers because of his background.

Despite these challenges, Mills remained determined and used his basketball talent, eventually gaining access to government sports programs that helped him develop his skills.

In several interviews, Mills has expressed his pride in his Aboriginal roots, saying, "My heritage and my culture, where I come from, mean everything to me."

This deep connection to his cultural identity has been a source of strength and motivation throughout his career.

On the court, Patrick Mills is known for his winning attitude and offensive mindset.

During his time with the San Antonio Spurs, he has been a key player in several crucial moments, especially during the playoffs.

His ability to score in tough situations and his leadership in the locker room have made him a favorite among both fans and his teammates.

In addition to his success in the NBA, Mills has been a leader and standout player on the international stage, helping Australia achieve its first Olympic medal in men's basketball (bronze) at the Tokyo 2020 Olympics.

38

Shawn Kemp

Born on November 26, 1969, in Elkhart, Indiana, Shawn Kemp is a former professional basketball player who had a remarkable 14-season career in the NBA.

Known for his impressive athletic ability, Kemp earned the nickname "Reign Man" during his time with the Seattle SuperSonics, where he reached the peak of his career.

However, his life on and off the court was marked by both achievements and controversies, making him a fascinating figure in basketball history.

From a very young age, Shawn Kemp displayed exceptional talent for basketball.

By the time he finished high school, he was considered one of the top five players in his class nationwide.

During his senior year at Concord High School, Kemp established himself as the leading scorer in Elkhart County, attracting the attention of numerous college recruiters.

He ultimately decided to attend the University of Kentucky, one of the top schools in college basketball.

However, a little-known fact is that Kemp did not achieve the minimum score of 700 points on the SAT, which disqualified him from playing in his freshman year due to NCAA rules.

This academic setback was an early indication of the challenges Kemp would face later in life. Kemp's time at the University of Kentucky was brief and controversial.

Although he couldn't play due to academic restrictions, he enrolled at the university with the hope of improving his grades.

Three months after his arrival, he became embroiled in a scandal when he was accused of stealing and pawning two gold chains that belonged to the son of Kentucky's coach, Eddie Sutton.

Although no formal charges were filed against him, Kemp was forced to leave the university and transfer to Trinity Valley Community College in Texas.

There, Kemp didn't have the opportunity to play basketball, and after one semester, he decided to drop out of school altogether, opting to enter the NBA draft directly.

Despite these early setbacks, Kemp was selected by the Seattle SuperSonics in the first round of the 1989 NBA Draft.

With the SuperSonics, Kemp quickly became a star, known for his impressive ability to execute spectacular dunks and his capacity to dominate the game on both ends of the court.

During his time in Seattle, he was selected six times for the All-Star Game and led the SuperSonics to the NBA Finals in 1996, where they ultimately lost to Michael Jordan's Chicago Bulls.

Off the court, Kemp's life was turbulent. He is known to have at least seven recognized children, though it is speculated that he may have more offspring who have not been officially acknowledged.

Additionally, Kemp faced numerous legal issues over the years, including several arrests for drug possession.

In one of these incidents, along with drugs, a semi-automatic pistol was also confiscated, adding more controversy to his already complicated personal life.

After retiring from the NBA in 2003, Kemp attempted to extend his professional career in European leagues, specifically in Italy, but was unsuccessful.

Despite these failed attempts to continue his career, Kemp devoted himself to other activities, including helping with the rehabilitation of Houston after Hurricane Ike in 2008.

This act of community service was an exemplary gesture that showed a more positive side of his character, contrasting with the problems he had faced earlier.

39

John Stockton

Born on March 26, 1962, in Spokane, Washington, John Stockton is widely recognized as one of the greatest point guards in NBA history.

Throughout his 19-year career in the league, all of which he spent with the Utah Jazz, Stockton excelled in his incredible ability to assist and steal the ball, achieving records that still stand today.

However, his life and career are filled with curiosities and details that make him a unique figure in professional basketball.

Stockton comes from a religious Irish family, and his calm and reserved demeanor reflects his upbringing.

Despite receiving offers from larger and more prestigious universities, he chose to attend Gonzaga University, which was just a few blocks from his home.

This attachment to his home and family was a constant in his life, demonstrating his focus on stability and community. Stockton is one of the few NBA players who completed his college education, graduating as a chiropractor.

This is notable, as many players leave college early to fully commit to professional basketball.

During his early years in college, Stockton did not initially stand out as a player.

He spent most of his time on the bench with limited minutes on the court.

However, over time, his dedication and work ethic led to significant improvement, eventually earning him a spot in the starting lineup.

Stockton was known for his reserved and introverted nature, as he disliked being the center of attention and maintained a low profile both on and off the court.

Despite not having many friends on his teams, he developed a strong camaraderie with Karl Malone, his teammate on the Utah Jazz.

This connection was crucial to his success in the NBA, as Stockton became the all-time leader in assists, largely due to his ability to assist Malone in pick-and-roll plays.

Throughout his NBA career, Stockton was underestimated in his early years.

He spent four years as a backup and was close to being cut from the team.

However, his dedication and consistency led him to become a starter and a key player for the Utah Jazz.

His discipline was remarkable; in 19 years, he missed only 23 games and was always the first to arrive at practices and games.

In his personal life, Stockton is a family man and leads a quiet private life.

He married the daughter of a governor of Alaska and has two daughters.

His Christian faith also plays a central role in his life. Stockton is a devout man, and his favorite book is the Bible, which he used to carry with him to games.

This practice contrasted with the image of other NBA players, who were known for their aggression and more extravagant lifestyles.

Throughout his career, Stockton remained true to his roots and style.

While NBA fashion shifted toward longer, baggier shorts in the 1990s, Stockton continued to wear short shorts in the style of the 1980s, earning him the nickname "Short Shorts."

Stockton retired in 2003, and the Utah Jazz honored him by erecting a statue in his honor outside the Delta Center, now Vivint Arena. They also named a street in Salt Lake City "John Stockton Drive."

Despite his success in the NBA, Stockton chose to step away from basketball after his retirement.

He did not become a coach or a sports commentator, preferring to dedicate his time to his family.

In the few interviews he has given, Stockton has mentioned that he might consider returning to basketball in some role once his children are grown.

In 1992, Stockton had the honor of being part of the legendary "Dream Team," the U.S. basketball team that won the gold medal at the Barcelona Olympics.

This team included iconic figures such as Michael Jordan, Magic Johnson, and Larry Bird, and is considered one of the greatest basketball teams of all time.

40

Gordon Hayward

Born on March 23, 1990, in Indianapolis, Indiana, Gordon Hayward is a prominent basketball player who has made a significant impact in the NBA.

Standing at 6'8" (2.03 meters) and playing as a forward, Hayward has been a key figure on the teams he has played for, including the Utah Jazz, where he established himself as one of the best players of the decade.

One of the most notable curiosities about Gordon Hayward is that he has a twin sister named Heather.

Unlike many twins who are the same sex, Gordon and Heather are fraternal twins.

Heather is not only his sister but also his best friend.

Despite the demands of his NBA career, Hayward maintains a very close relationship with Heather and always makes sure to stay in touch with her, no matter where he is or how busy he may be.

Hayward has mentioned in several interviews that he couldn't imagine his life without her.

Another interesting fact about Gordon Hayward is that he is the tallest member of his family.

His parents, who are approximately 5'10" (1.78 meters) tall, noticed his large size even when he was a baby.

From an early age, both Gordon and his sister Heather participated in sports, which helped them develop their coordination and agility.

Given his height, Gordon naturally gravitated toward basketball, a sport in which he quickly excelled thanks to his skill and physique.

In addition to his success on the court, Gordon Hayward is a dedicated father and an avid video game player.

He is married to Robyn Hayward, and together they have a daughter named Bernadette Marie Hayward.

An interesting anecdote about Hayward is that when his daughter was a newborn, he could often be seen taking care of her while playing video games, specifically League of Legends, one of his favorite games.

A viral image on social media shows Hayward playing on his computer with his daughter in his lap, combining his parenting responsibilities with his passion for video games.

His teammate Rudy Gobert captured and shared the photo, giving fans a glimpse of this more personal and fun side of Hayward.

Regarding his love for video games, Hayward is an extremely competitive player, not just on the court but also in the virtual world.

On one occasion, he wrote a provocative statement on his blog in which he declared himself the best gamer in the world.

In his post, he challenged the best players in the NBA, claiming that he could beat them even if they all teamed up against him.

Although this made some people think he had lost his mind, Hayward clarified that he was talking about League of Legends, his true second passion.

His love for video games is so strong that he has even considered the possibility of pursuing a career in eSports after retiring from basketball.

41

Metta World Peace

Formerly known as Ron Artest, Metta World Peace is one of the most controversial and unique players in NBA history.

Born on November 13, 1979, in Queens, New York, Artest had an NBA career filled with highs and lows, characterized by both his talent on the court and his numerous incidents off it.

Known for his relentless defense and intensity, Artest was also an eccentric character, creating several unforgettable moments both inside and outside of basketball.

One of the most curious anecdotes about Metta World Peace is how he celebrated his contract with the Los Angeles Lakers.

Instead of opting for a luxurious party or a traditional event, he decided to organize a Monopoly game on the beach with several Lakers fans.

This event reflects his unique personality and love for board games.

In addition to Monopoly, Metta is a fan of checkers and claims to have never lost a game, showcasing his competitiveness even in activities outside of basketball.

In a remarkable act of generosity, Metta World Peace decided to auction off his NBA championship ring that he won with the Lakers in 2010.

The auction raised $100,000, which he then distributed between two children's foundations in New York.

This gesture exemplified his altruistic side, as he chose to use one of his most cherished achievements to help others.

Throughout his career, Metta World Peace was known for his physical and intense style of play.

This approach led to several tough encounters, including one with Michael Jordan during a practice.

In that matchup, Metta faced Jordan in a one-on-one, and in his attempt to compete at the highest level, he ended up cracking two of the basketball legend's ribs.

This incident clearly illustrates the intensity with which Metta played, even in practices.

One of the strangest moments in Metta World Peace's career occurred in January 2004, when he showed up to practice wearing nothing but a bathrobe.

When asked why he did this, he explained that he wanted to remind himself to "take it easier."

This episode is just one of the many eccentricities that defined his personality off the court.

Metta World Peace is perhaps best known for his involvement in one of the most infamous brawls in NBA history: the fight between the Indiana Pacers and the Detroit Pistons in 2004, commonly referred to as "The Malice at the Palace."

This brawl involved both players and fans and had serious consequences for everyone involved.

Metta was suspended for 72 games, the longest suspension for a non-drug-related incident in NBA history, and he was fined nearly $5 million.

This event deeply affected his reputation and career, but it also marked a turning point in his personal and professional life.

Outside of basketball, Metta World Peace ventured into the world of hip-hop.

He performed live at several nightclubs in New York and Los Angeles and appeared in the music video for the song "Nas is Like" by rapper Nas in 1999.

This side of him shows his interest in music and his desire to explore other creative areas beyond basketball.

Metta World Peace is also known for his multiple name changes.

In 2011, he legally changed his name from Ron Artest to Metta World Peace as part of an effort to promote peace and kindness.

However, in 2014, he changed his name again, this time to "The Panda's Friend" during his stint in Chinese basketball.

On another occasion, he considered the name "Max Power," inspired by an episode of "The Simpsons."

These name changes reflect his whimsical personality and his constant search for reinvention.

42

Patrick Ewing

Patrick Aloysius Ewing is a basketball legend, born on August 5, 1962, in Kingston, Jamaica.

Despite his Jamaican roots, Ewing was raised in the United States, where he became one of the most iconic players in NBA history.

His career was marked by his dominance on the court, especially as the center for the New York Knicks, and his imposing style of play that made him a 4 feared force in the league.

One of the most touching anecdotes about Patrick Ewing occurred in 2000 when his on-court rival and close friend, Alonzo Mourning, was diagnosed with a severe kidney disease that required an urgent transplant.

Ewing, demonstrating immense camaraderie and generosity, voluntarily offered to donate one of his kidneys to Mourning.

Although tests showed that Ewing was not the most compatible donor, the gesture did not go unnoticed.

Eventually, a relative of Mourning turned out to be a better candidate for the transplant, but Ewing's willingness to help his friend in such a critical moment reflects the human quality that defines him.

In addition to his success on the court, Patrick Ewing also ventured into the world of film.

His popularity as a player and his charismatic presence caught the attention of Hollywood, which led to his appearances in several films.

One of his most notable roles was in The Exorcist III, where he played the character "The Angel of Death."

He also made a brief cameo in the iconic Warner Brothers animated film Space Jam, alongside other NBA stars like Michael Jordan and Charles Barkley.

These appearances on the big screen expanded his fame beyond basketball, showcasing his versatility and ability to stand out in different areas.

Patrick Ewing's number 33 is another symbol of his legacy.

After retiring in 2002, the New York Knicks, the team with which he spent most of his career, paid him a special tribute.

In an emotional event held at Madison Square Garden in 2003, the number 33 was officially retired, hanging high in the stadium as a permanent tribute to his impact on the team and the city of New York.

This honor ensures that his legacy will endure in the memories of fans and that his contribution to basketball will never be forgotten.

Before becoming the basketball superstar we all know, Patrick Ewing had other athletic interests.

As a child in Jamaica, he practiced cricket and was fascinated by European soccer, but he had no knowledge of basketball until he moved to the United States in 1973, at the age of 13.

It was in Cambridge, Massachusetts, where Ewing began playing basketball, discovering a natural talent that would lead him to become one of the greatest players in NBA history.

Ewing is widely regarded as one of the most important players in the NBA and is a member of the Basketball Hall of Fame.

Throughout his career, he was selected 11 times for the All-Star Game, was named to the All-NBA First Team twice, and established himself as one of the best defensive centers of his era.

His dominance on the court, combined with his work ethic and leadership, places him among the 50 greatest players in NBA history, a list that recognizes the most influential and successful players in the sport.

43

Rajon Rondo

Born on February 22, 1986, in Louisville, Kentucky, Rajon Rondo is a professional basketball player known for his defensive prowess, speed, and agility on the court, as well as his strong personality.

From a young age, Rondo showed an interest in sports, particularly in American football.

However, his mother, Amber Rondo, was concerned about the risk of injuries due to his slender build and convinced him to switch to basketball, a sport in which he quickly excelled.

This change marked the beginning of a career that would lead him to the NBA, where he would become one of the best point guards of his generation.

Rondo's life wasn't easy from the start.

When he was seven years old, his father left the family, leaving his mother to raise Rajon and his three siblings on her own.

Amber Rondo worked the third shift at Philip Morris USA, making significant sacrifices to support her family.

This difficult environment instilled in Rondo a determination and mental toughness that would be crucial in his career.

One of the most painful moments in Rondo's life occurred during his final year in college, before entering the NBA draft.

His best friend, Spencer Ronson, was brutally murdered, an event that deeply affected Rondo.

The loss was devastating, and those who knew him noticed a change in his behavior.

However, Rondo found solace in basketball, using the sport as an outlet to channel his pain.

In honor of his friend, he got a tattoo on his back, keeping his memory alive every time he stepped onto the court.

Rondo is also a person of faith and attributes his success not only to his hard work and dedication but also to his belief in God.

This faith has provided him with a solid foundation and a source of strength throughout his life and career.

On the court, Rondo is known for his fierce competitiveness and relentless focus.

His friends and colleagues describe him as a kind and humble person off the court, but when he's in the game, he transforms into an unstoppable competitor who isn't afraid to take on anyone.

This duality in his personality, along with his innate talent, has been key to his success in the NBA.

Throughout his career, Rondo has experienced both highs and lows as well as moments of glory.

Despite the adversities he has faced, he has always chosen light over darkness, using his challenges as motivation to reach new heights.

44

David Lee

Born on April 29, 1983, in St. Louis, Missouri, David Lee is a former American basketball player who excelled in the NBA as a power forward.

Throughout his career, Lee played for several major teams, including the New York Knicks, Golden State Warriors, Boston Celtics, and San Antonio Spurs.

Although his career was filled with achievements, his reserved personality and modest playing style made him one of the most underrated players of his generation.

One of the most interesting aspects of David Lee's career is how he became ambidextrous.

Originally, Lee was entirely left-handed, but during his childhood, he suffered a fracture in his left arm, forcing him to use his right arm for an extended period.

This setback turned out to be a blessing in disguise, as it allowed him to develop the ability to use both arms with equal skill in basketball, a quality that became one of his strengths on the court.

Despite his large size and presence on the court, David Lee is known for being extremely shy and reserved.

This shyness was evident from his childhood, making it difficult for him to form lasting relationships and friendships.

According to his parents, Gary and Susan Lee, David preferred to observe and learn rather than socialize.

His mother described him as "a walking sponge," always absorbing knowledge from his surroundings.

This introversion also influenced his initial choice of sports; he started playing tennis because it allowed him to compete individually without the pressure of interacting with a team.

Throughout his NBA career, David Lee was consistently underrated, despite his impressive statistics and performance.

He rarely received the recognition he deserved, as his playing style prioritized teamwork over individual stardom, and his quiet personality contributed to him being overlooked even during moments of great success.

For example, during his time with the New York Knicks, despite being one of the team's most consistent players, his personal life remained a mystery to most.

Donnie Walsh, the Knicks' owner, commented in 2012 that almost no one knew anything about Lee off the court, highlighting an incident where Lee only approached the team to inform them that he needed to catch a flight because his grandfather had passed away.

Despite being underestimated, Lee managed to build a respectable NBA career.

He was selected for the All-Star Game twice and was part of the Golden State Warriors team that won the NBA championship in 2015.

However, his path was not without difficulties, as he faced several injuries throughout his career that forced him to constantly fight to maintain his place in the league.

Despite these challenges, his dedication and professionalism made him a respected veteran in the league.

45

Wilt Chamberlain

Wilt Chamberlain is one of the most iconic and dominant figures in the history of basketball.

Born on August 21, 1936, in Philadelphia, Pennsylvania, Chamberlain left an indelible mark on the NBA with his impressive statistics, athletic abilities, and unmatched records.

Throughout his career, Chamberlain redefined what it meant to be a basketball player, setting records that, to this day, remain nearly unbreakable.

In 1996, Wilt Chamberlain was selected as one of the 50 greatest players in NBA history, ranking 15th on the list.

This recognition was based on his impressive career, which included two NBA championships and four MVP awards.

Chamberlain's inclusion in this prestigious list solidified his legacy as one of the greatest of all time.

Chamberlain is undoubtedly the player with the most records in NBA history, with an astonishing total of 72.

Among his most notable achievements is scoring 100 points in a single game, a record that has remained unbroken since 1962.

Additionally, he is the only player in NBA history to have averaged 30 points and 20 rebounds per game throughout his career, a feat that underscores his dominance on the court and unparalleled athletic ability.

Like many athletes of his caliber, Chamberlain had several nicknames throughout his life. Some of the most well-known include "The Big Dipper," "Goliath," "Chalmers," and "Wilt The Stilt."

Interestingly, although "Wilt The Stilt" is one of the most famous nicknames, Chamberlain hated it because he felt it referred to his height in a derogatory way.

After retiring from basketball in 1973, Chamberlain pursued a variety of business ventures.

He distanced himself from basketball as a coach and decided to open a popular nightclub in Harlem called Smalls Paradise.

He also made lucrative investments in real estate in Los Angeles and sponsored volleyball and track and field teams.

These investments made him a multimillionaire, demonstrating that his success was not limited to the basketball courts.

One of the most controversial aspects of Chamberlain's life was revealed in his second autobiography, where he claimed to have had sexual relations with approximately 20,000 women.

This confession generated a great deal of criticism and controversy, but Chamberlain defended his lifestyle, saying he was simply doing "something natural" and that he made sure not to get involved with married women.

Despite his very active love life, he was never known to have any children, and he remained publicly single.

In the last years of his life, Chamberlain suffered from health problems, primarily related to his heart.

Although he was under treatment, he passed away on October 12, 1999, at the age of 63 due to a sudden heart attack while sleeping.

His death was a blow to the sports world, but his legacy remains intact.

In addition to his basketball talent, Chamberlain was an exceptional athlete in other sports.

During his youth, he excelled as an all-around athlete, even high jumping 6 feet 6 inches (1.98 meters) in track and field competitions.

His overall athletic ability was so impressive that many consider him one of the greatest athletes of all time, not just in basketball.

46

Chris Mullin.

Born on July 30, 1963, in Brooklyn, New York, he is one of the most prominent figures in NBA history.

His career, full of achievements and challenges, positions him as a player who left an indelible mark on basketball.

Known for his scoring ability, court intelligence, and precise shooting, Mullin was an icon both on and off the court.

Although he retired in 2001, his legacy lives on in the NBA and among fans.

One of the most iconic aspects of Chris Mullin is his choice of the number 17 for his jersey.

This number was not chosen at random but was a tribute to his childhood hero, John "Hondo" Havlicek, a Boston Celtics legend.

Mullin grew up admiring Havlicek and decided to honor him by wearing his number, a gesture that reflects the profound influence Havlicek had on his life and career.

However, Mullin's life was not without difficulties.

During his career, he battled serious alcoholism issues that nearly ended his time in the NBA.

The situation became so severe that Mullin had to leave basketball for over a year to enter a rehabilitation clinic.

This period was crucial for his life because, after overcoming his addiction, he returned to basketball with renewed determination and discipline, allowing him to continue his career at the highest level.

Regarding his achievements on the court, Mullin was selected five times to participate in the NBA All-Star Game, an honor reserved only for the best players in the league.

This accomplishment underscores his status as one of the greats of his generation.

Additionally, Mullin was part of the legendary trio known as Run TMC, along with Tim Hardaway and Mitch Richmond, on the Golden State Warriors.

This trio was characterized by their fast and offensive style of play, revolutionizing basketball in their era.

Mullin's precision in shooting is another of his most outstanding features.

Throughout his career, he was known for his ability to score with unmatched accuracy, making him a true scoring machine. To this day, few players have come close to his record in field goal accuracy.

On the international stage, Chris Mullin also left his mark.

He is the second player in NBA history to win two Olympic gold medals, achieved at the Los Angeles 1984 and Barcelona 1992 Olympic Games.

The second medal was won as a member of the iconic 1992 "Dream Team," considered by many to be the greatest basketball team of all time.

The first player to achieve two gold medals in basketball was Michael Jordan, who was also part of the Dream Team and is well-known for his role in the movie "Space Jam."

Despite his personal struggles, Mullin managed to overcome his challenges and return to basketball stronger than ever.

In 1989, after his battle with alcoholism, he returned to the NBA and quickly established himself as one of the league's best shooters.

His ability to overcome adversity and his dedication to the game earned him the respect and admiration of his teammates, coaches, and fans.

47

Paul Pierce.

Born on October 13, 1977, in Oakland, California, he is one of the most notable basketball legends, known by his nickname "The Truth," which was given to him by none other than Shaquille O'Neal after a matchup between the Boston Celtics and the Los Angeles Lakers.

This nickname reflects his ability to excel in critical moments and his honesty on the court, where he earned the respect of both teammates and opponents.

Pierce reached one of the highest points of his career in 2008 when he led the Boston Celtics to an NBA championship victory.

It was a historic season for the team, and Pierce was awarded the NBA Finals MVP, solidifying himself as the best player in the decisive series.

This achievement was the culmination of years of effort and dedication, placing him among the greats in the history of the league.

Pierce's story is not without challenges.

He grew up in Inglewood, a suburb of Los Angeles known for its high crime rate.

His childhood was marked by street violence and the absence of his father, leaving his single mother solely responsible for raising Paul and his siblings.

Despite this adverse environment, Pierce found refuge and an outlet in basketball.

He practiced daily, and his talent did not go unnoticed; he was discovered by Scott Collins, a local coach, who saw extraordinary potential in him and helped channel his energy into the sport.

One of the most impactful events in Pierce's life occurred in 2000 when he was the victim of a brutal attack at a nightclub in Boston.

He was stabbed 11 times and severely beaten, putting not only his career but also his life at risk.

Amazingly, Pierce not only survived but also made a full recovery and returned to the court shortly afterward.

The most incredible part of this incident is that during his treatment, his only concern was whether his arms—his most valuable tools as a player—had remained unharmed.

This episode demonstrated his incredible mental strength and dedication to basketball.

In his personal life, Pierce is known for his love and dedication to his family.

An example of this is the curious gift he gave his daughter Jazzy for her fifth birthday.

The little girl had asked for a llama, an unusual request, but Pierce didn't hesitate to fulfill her wish.

During the birthday party, he made a spectacular entrance by bringing in the animal, fulfilling one of his daughter's dreams and showing his most eccentric and affectionate side.

48

Drazen Petrovic.

Born on October 22, 1964, in Šibenik, Croatia, he is remembered as one of the greatest European basketball players of all time and a legend who left an indelible mark on NBA history.

His tragic death in a car accident in 1993 cut short a career that promised even more greatness.

Petrovic was not only a pioneer for European players in the NBA but also a global basketball icon known for his skill, passion, and competitive spirit.

The player had a unique way of motivating himself during games.

He was known for quietly singing a peculiar chant: "son of a b****," a phrase often hurled at him by rival fans.

Instead of letting the insults affect him, he used these words as a mantra to stay focused and fired up during matches.

Interestingly, Drazen Petrovic was almost named Robert.

His parents considered this option to honor former U.S. President John F. Kennedy, but in the end, on his grandmother's advice, they decided to name him Drazen, a Yugoslav name meaning "beautiful" or "affectionate."

This name, along with his talent, would become synonymous with greatness in basketball.

From a young age, Petrovic demonstrated unwavering determination.

Along with his brother Aleksandar and other friends, he would often play basketball late into the night on a street called Preradovic.

One day, a neighbor, annoyed by the noise, broke the basketball hoop to stop them from playing.

The next day, the boys installed another hoop and, in an act of revenge, threw a dynamite cartridge into the neighbor's yard.

This anecdote reflects the persistent and rebellious character that defined Drazen throughout his life.

As for his NBA career, Petrovic always knew he wanted to be one of the best three-point shooters in the league.

That's why he chose the number 3 for his jersey, symbolizing his ambition to dominate three-point shooting.

His hard work paid off, as he became one of the best three-point shooters in the NBA, finishing his career as the fourth-highest three-point percentage shooter in the league's history at that time.

Petrovic's talent was not unique in his family.

In addition to his brother Aleksandar, his second cousin Dejan Bodiroga also stood out as one of the best basketball players of the 1990s, playing for teams like FC Barcelona and Real Madrid.

Petrovic's fame did not diminish after his death.

In Zagreb, his hometown, the Cibona arena was renamed the "Drazen Petrovic Basketball Hall" in his honor.

Additionally, a museum dedicated to his life and career was inaugurated, and a street in Zagreb bears his name, perpetuating his legacy in his country and around the world.

One of the most surprising anecdotes occurred in 1987 during a game between Yugoslavia and the United States.

In the midst of an attempted fight between several players, including Drazen, his mother, Biserka Petrovic, jumped on to the court and, with a cane in hand, tried to defend her son by hitting other players.

This event highlights the deep family bond and the protective nature of his mother.

49

Jason Kidd.

He is one of the most iconic figures in the NBA, with a career spanning from 1994 to 2013, leaving an indelible mark on basketball.

Standing at 1.94 meters tall, Kidd was known for his playing style, leadership, and on-court skills, leading the teams he played for to the top of the NBA on multiple occasions.

Throughout his career, Kidd was selected 10 times to participate in the NBA All-Star Game, an achievement that very few players can boast.

This accomplishment reflects his ability to stand out among the best and his impact on the league.

One of the most interesting facts about Jason Kidd is that, in his childhood, his true passion was not basketball, but soccer.

For years, Kidd leaned towards this sport and showed little interest in basketball.

However, over time, he changed course and decided to dedicate himself to basketball, a decision that undoubtedly shaped the history of the sport.

It's intriguing to imagine what his career might have been like if he had continued with soccer.

Kidd grew up in Oakland, California, just like another basketball legend, Gary Payton.

Both encountered each other on the courts and parks of the city during their childhood, a coincidence that resulted in the formation of two of the most outstanding players in the NBA.

Throughout his career, Kidd has always declared himself a big fan of Ricky Rubio, the talented Spanish point guard, showing his admiration for the young player's style of play.

After retiring from basketball in 2013, Kidd took on a new challenge as the coach of the Brooklyn Nets, a team he had played for as a player. However, his coaching career was not limited to the Nets, as he later took the helm of the Milwaukee Bucks, where he also made his mark as a leader.

Kidd made his NBA debut with the Dallas Mavericks, where he quickly showcased his potential.

In his first game, he nearly achieved his first triple-double, scoring 10 points, dishing out 11 assists, and grabbing 8 rebounds.

This initial performance was a sign of the successful career that would follow.

Kidd remains one of the most prolific players in terms of double-doubles and triple-doubles, in addition to accumulating an impressive amount of minutes played throughout his career.

His impact was so significant that both the University of California and the Brooklyn Nets decided to retire the number 5 jersey in his honor, a recognition reserved only for the greats of the sport.

One of Jason Kidd's most well-known quirks is his free-throw ritual.

He used to kiss the fingers of his right hand and blow a kiss into the air before taking the shot.

This gesture became a distinctive symbol of Kidd, but few know its origin.

This ritual began after Kidd was found guilty of assaulting his wife.

As an act of repentance, he started performing this gesture as a public way of asking for forgiveness for what had happened, serving as a constant reminder of his commitment to change and redemption.

50

Clyde Drexler.

He is a former NBA player who is widely remembered and admired not only in the United States but also around the world.

Throughout his career, Drexler left an indelible mark on basketball history, accumulating historic numbers, representing his country in international competitions, and earning the honor of being inducted into the Basketball Hall of Fame.

One of the most interesting aspects of Drexler is that during his time at the University of Houston, he created a basketball fraternity known as "Phi Slamma Jamma."

This fraternity stood out for its members' skills in jumping and aerial dunks, which helped Drexler develop his own style and stand out from an early stage.

His nickname, "The Glide," is a reflection of his incredible ability to move smoothly on the court.

Drexler was known for his speed, muscular build, and ability to appear unexpectedly and decisively in plays, successfully finishing many of them.

This nickname perfectly captured his elegant and effective playing style.

Interestingly, basketball was not always his favorite sport.

During his childhood and adolescence, Drexler preferred playing baseball, and it was only due to the insistence of his best friend that he finally decided to join the basketball team in his senior year of high school.

This decision, driven by his friend's influence, was a turning point that would lead him to a legendary career in the NBA.

In addition to his success on the court, Drexler has a special connection to the culinary world.

His family owns a well-known chain of restaurants in Houston called "Drexler's World Famous BBQ & Grill."

Since Clyde Drexler achieved fame, these restaurants have become popular tourist destinations, attracting both basketball fans and food lovers.

In 1996, Drexler was named one of the 50 greatest players in NBA history, surpassing stars such as Julius Erving, Patrick Ewing, and George Gervin.

This recognition solidified his status as one of the basketball greats.

Finally, in 2004, he was inducted into the Basketball Hall of Fame in the United States, an honor that crowned his nearly 20 years of impeccable career and his historic contributions to the sport.

51

Vince Carter.

Known for his impressive basketball skills, he is a legendary figure who has left an indelible mark on the NBA.

Beyond his outstanding sports career, there are many fascinating aspects of his life and personality that make him even more interesting.

One of the most notable aspects of Vince Carter is his numerous nicknames, which reflect his talent and charisma in the game.

Nicknames like "Air Canada," "Vinsanity," "The King Air," "Half Man, Half Amazing," and "Invenceable" highlight his ability to amaze fans with his spectacular playing style, especially during his time with the Toronto Raptors, where he won the NBA Rookie of the Year title.

Carter was influenced from a young age by his uncle Oliver Lee, who was also a basketball player, but his greatest inspiration was Julius Erving, known as "Dr. J."

Carter grew up mimicking Erving's moves, who was his idol and role model.

This influence was key in developing his playing style, known for his acrobatic dunks and his ability to soar above the competition.

Vince Carter's personal life also has interesting stories.

His biological father abandoned him when he was a child, and although he reconnected with him later, Carter considers Harry Robinson, who married his mother, to be his true father.

Robinson was not only a father figure but also taught Vince to play various musical instruments, such as the drums, trumpet, and saxophone, which sparked his love for music.

Carter even participated in musical groups, showing that his talent was not limited to basketball.

Regarding his academic and athletic career, Carter was highly sought after by several universities, but he ultimately chose the University of North Carolina, where he continued to hone his skills.

His self-discipline was remarkable, as after a loss in the second round of the NCAA tournament in 1996, Carter stayed on campus all summer practicing his technique, determined to improve for the next season.

Vince Carter's impact was not only limited to his fans but also extended to other players.

Kobe Bryant, one of the NBA's biggest stars, admitted that Carter was one of his main sources of inspiration during his high school years, a testament to the respect Carter earned among his peers and rivals.

In his personal life, Carter married Ellen Rucker, a chiropractor he met in college, in 2004.

They had a daughter named Kai Michelle Carter, and although the marriage ended in 2006, Carter and Rucker maintain an excellent friendship.

52

Brandon Roy.

Born in 1984, he is a former American basketball player who made a significant impact in the NBA despite his short career.

Roy debuted in the league with the Portland Trail Blazers in 2006, where he quickly stood out for his exceptional ball-handling skills and his ability to lead his team in critical situations.

In his debut game, he scored 20 points, a glimpse of what would be his promising career in the league.

Between 2008 and 2010, Roy averaged over 20 points per game and maintained a free-throw percentage above 80%.

His on-court prowess led to comparisons with some of the biggest stars in the NBA.

One of his most memorable moments came in 2008 when he scored 52 points against the Phoenix Suns, setting a personal record and demonstrating his ability to dominate a game.

However, Roy's success was short-lived due to a series of severe knee injuries.

Throughout his career, he underwent seven surgeries to treat his joint problems, which forced him to play with knee braces to protect himself and conceal the scars.

Despite his perseverance and desire to keep playing, persistent injuries led to a devastating diagnosis: if he continued to play, he risked ending up in a wheelchair.

In 2011, Roy announced his retirement from basketball, citing concerns for his health and his desire to be present for his son, Brandon Jr., who was born in 2007.

Despite his retirement, Roy attempted a comeback to the NBA in 2012 after undergoing experimental plasma injection treatment in his knees, which allowed for brief improvement.

However, the injuries returned, and he was forced to retire for good.

Currently, Brandon Roy has found a new passion in teaching and coaching basketball.

He serves as a coach at the Nathan Hale High School basketball academy in Seattle, his hometown, where he also maintains strong ties with childhood friends.

Roy has expressed interest in returning to the NBA, this time as a coach, and is using his experience in youth categories to develop his skills in team management.

53

Jimmy Butler.

He is a basketball player who has captured the attention of fans not only for his skill on the court but also for his personal story and charisma.

At 27 years old, he has become a key figure in the NBA, especially known for his time with the Chicago Bulls.

However, what truly sets Butler apart is not just his statistics but his incredible story of overcoming adversity and the interesting facts surrounding him.

Jimmy Butler's life has been marked by hardship from a very young age.

Orphaned by his father, he was abandoned by his mother at the age of 13, who told him she didn't like his appearance and kicked him out of the house.

This situation left him virtually homeless, forcing him to sleep at friends' houses and move around constantly.

But his life took a turn when he met Jordan Leslie, another basketball player at his high school.

After challenging each other in a dunk contest, Butler and Leslie formed a bond so strong that Jordan's mother, despite already having four children, decided to take Jimmy into her home.

Since then, Jimmy considers Jordan a brother, even though they don't share blood ties.

Interestingly, Jordan Leslie has also made a notable career, but in the NFL with the Atlanta Falcons.

Jimmy Butler has a character and life philosophy that are reflected in his decisions and way of living.

One of his most well-known anecdotes is that he decided to remove the rearview mirror from his car to remind himself never to look back, a metaphor that speaks to his focus on the present and future.

He also has an unusual passion for music.

Beyond simply enjoying music, Butler took this passion to another level by hiring the designers from the show "Tanked" to build a fish tank in his home in the shape of a boombox, a clear demonstration of his love for music and his desire to keep it present in his daily life.

Among his close friends is the famous actor Mark Wahlberg, with whom he has developed a friendship that surprises many.

These kinds of connections and his charisma have made Jimmy Butler a respected and beloved figure both on and off the court.

Despite all the challenges he has faced, Butler has become one of the NBA's brightest stars, known for his dedication, work ethic, and ability to overcome any obstacle.

Nicknamed "Jimmy G Buckets" by commentator Stacey King, Butler continues to demonstrate his passion for basketball, leading his teams with determination and an indomitable spirit.

54

Chandler Parsons.

Born in 1988, he is an NBA player who has made his mark both on and off the court.

Since entering the league in 2012, he has played for teams such as the Houston Rockets and the Dallas Mavericks.

Known for his ability to score from long range, Parsons has earned a reputation as an excellent three-point shooter, particularly when he broke a record by making 10 three-pointers in the second half of a game against the Memphis Grizzlies.

This achievement cemented his place as a notable player in terms of perimeter shooting accuracy.

However, his performance on the court has been the subject of criticism.

Despite his ability to score threes, many consider him an inconsistent player, often coming off the bench and lacking the level of consistency expected from a star in the NBA.

Even so, his popularity extends beyond his athletic performance.

Parsons has attracted significant attention, especially among female fans, due to his looks and his love life.

He is known for his relationships with famous models and celebrities, which has increased his notoriety outside of basketball.

Among his most notable relationships is Kendall Jenner, one of the most recognized figures in the world of modeling and television, famous for her participation in the Kardashian reality show.

Parsons has also been linked to Toni Garrn, a prominent German model who previously dated actor Leonardo DiCaprio.

These relationships have kept Parsons in the media spotlight, not just for his game but also for his social life.

In addition to his basketball career, Chandler Parsons has also ventured into the world of modeling, which has helped increase his social media following, especially on Instagram, where he has millions of fans, mostly women.

This dual role as an athlete and model has made Parsons a figure who transcends sports, blending the rigor of the NBA with the glamour of entertainment and fashion.

55

Monta Ellis.

He is a basketball player who has captured the attention and admiration of many due to his exceptional skills on the court.

His sports career is well known, but his life outside of basketball is also filled with interesting facts.

For example, his name has a special origin: the correct pronunciation is "Mon-tei," derived from Montana, the name of his grandfather, whom his mother wanted to honor.

Ellis has a very close idol, his older brother Antwain, whom he always admired as the best basketball player he knew.

In their neighborhood, Antwain was compared to Tracy McGrady, and Monta learned a lot from him in his early days.

However, Antwain stopped playing basketball after losing a close friend, which led Monta to double down on his efforts in the sport, drawing inspiration from legends like Michael Jordan and Kobe Bryant, whose moves he tried to emulate.

In 2008, Monta Ellis faced a setback when an accident at home during a workout caused a serious injury to the ligaments in his left knee, sidelining him for 30 games.

This incident demonstrated the pressure and self-discipline he subjected himself to in his pursuit of perfection.

Ellis is also known for his striking tattoos, among which a family tree on his torso stands out, symbolizing the importance of family.

On his back, he carries the logo of the Golden State Warriors, the team that discovered him and gave him the opportunity to shine in the NBA.

He also has other meaningful tattoos, such as a portrait of himself as a child, the number 72, his initials, a dove, and more, turning his body into a true gallery of personal art.

A curious detail about Monta Ellis is his unique ritual of dipping his hands in hot wax before going out to play.

According to him, this helps improve his shooting, highlighting his focus on performance and the superstition surrounding his game preparation.

In his personal life, Monta married Juanika Ellis in 2011, with whom he has two children, Monta Ellis Jr. and Myla Jai Ellis.

Throughout his career, Ellis has expressed pride in overcoming numerous adversities to achieve his goals.

In an interview, he mentioned, "I am happy. If you knew everything I've been through to get here, it was horrible, but every sacrifice deserves a reward. I feel proud."

Monta Ellis is a clear example of how effort and determination can lead a person to overcome any obstacle on the path to success, both in sports and in life.

56

Charles Barkley.

He is a former NBA player who, over his 16-year career, stood out for his impressive talent and skill on the court.

His legacy in basketball is such that he is considered one of the 50 greatest players in NBA history.

While his basketball career is widely known, there are curious and notable aspects about Barkley that not everyone may know.

One of Barkley's greatest achievements was being part of the legendary "Dream Team" at the 1992 Olympic Games, the U.S. basketball team that dominated in Barcelona and is considered one of the best teams ever assembled in any sport.

Additionally, Barkley was selected for the All-Star Game 11 times, a feat that places him among the league's most outstanding players.

Off the court, Barkley also had interests in politics.

In 1995, he joined the Republican Party, and in 1998, he considered running for the position of Governor of Alabama.

Although he ultimately did not pursue a political career, his interest in the political arena revealed a different side of his personality.

One of the lesser-known but quite notable characteristics of Barkley is his problem with gambling.

Over the years, he has lost large sums of money to gambling, a weakness he has openly admitted.

Barkley is also known for his appearance in the children's movie *Space Jam* alongside Michael Jordan.

In the film, Barkley, along with other NBA players, temporarily loses his ability to play basketball due to an alien plot.

This appearance in *Space Jam* further solidified his celebrity status outside the sports world.

In 2006, his outstanding NBA career was recognized when he was inducted into the Basketball Hall of Fame, an honor reserved for the greatest players of all time.

One of the most curious and talked-about aspects of Barkley throughout his career was his weight.

Since his high school days, Barkley struggled with being overweight, leading many to underestimate his potential on the court.

However, his talent was so evident that even at Auburn University, he was described as "a fat guy… who plays like the wind."

His weight, combined with his height and skill, earned him the nickname "The Round Mound of Rebound."

57

Tyson Chandler.

He is a prominent NBA player, primarily recognized for his skill as a center.

From a very young age, Chandler showed a deep love for basketball.

Raised on a farm with his mother, grandfather, and siblings, Chandler grew up practicing this sport as part of his daily activities.

One of the most significant moments of his childhood was when his grandfather, Cleotis, gave him his first basketball at the age of three and built a hoop on a tree at the entrance of their home.

This basketball remains one of his most treasured possessions.

As for his personal tastes, Chandler is a big fan of Mexican food.

Whenever he travels to Mexico, he gets excited about enjoying his favorite dishes, particularly street tacos, corn, and beans.

He also enjoys the characteristic spiciness of Mexican cuisine.

Despite his success in the NBA, Chandler did not have an easy childhood.

During his school years, he was bullied because of his height, which caused him frustration and led him to skip school on several occasions.

This bullying was a significant factor in his mother's decision to move to California with him and his siblings, seeking a more favorable environment for his development.

In addition to his basketball career, Chandler has also ventured into the world of modeling.

On one occasion, he posed nude for ESPN magazine's "Hot Body Issue," showcasing his confidence and comfort with his body.

In his neighborhood, Chandler was both admired and envied.

His great height and charisma made him the center of attention, especially among the neighborhood girls.

This popularity made him stand out not only as a promising athlete but also as the "neighborhood sensation."

Regarding his personal life, Tyson Chandler has maintained a strong relationship with his wife, Kimberly Chandler, who was his lifelong girlfriend.

Together, they have three children and are deeply committed to charitable causes, contributing donations and collaborating with various institutions to help those in need.

58

Andrew Wiggins

At 22 years old, he is one of the rising stars in professional basketball, standing out for his impressive skill on the court.

Born in Canada and standing 2.03 meters tall, Wiggins is known in the basketball world as "The Messiah," a nickname that reflects his talent and potential in the NBA.

Despite his young age, Wiggins has earned the respect and admiration of both his teammates and basketball fans.

This recognition is due not only to his performance on the court but also to his interesting background and the intriguing facts surrounding him.

Wiggins comes from a family deeply connected to sports, particularly basketball.

His father, Mitchell Wiggins, was a former NBA player, and his older brothers also excelled in the sport, which contributed to Andrew developing a strong passion for basketball from a very young age.

This family influence was crucial to his development as a player and his rise to the elite of world basketball.

One of the most notable anecdotes in Wiggins' career is that he was selected as the number one pick in the 2014 NBA Draft by the Cleveland Cavaliers, an honor reserved for the most promising players.

However, before even playing a game with the Cavaliers, Wiggins was part of a trade that sent him to the Minnesota Timberwolves, making him the second player in NBA history to be selected as the first overall pick in the Draft and then traded before making his debut.

Wiggins' athletic ability comes not only from his father but also from his mother, Marita Payne Wiggins, a renowned Canadian athlete.

This combination of athletic genes has allowed Andrew to excel in the NBA, not only for his scoring ability but also for his versatility, as he can play both small forward and shooting guard, making him a very valuable player for any team.

Throughout his early seasons, Wiggins was criticized for his inconsistent outside shooting.

However, instead of getting discouraged, he worked hard to improve his technique, seeking support from his coaches and teammates.

This dedication paid off in later seasons, where his outside shooting became much more effective, demonstrating his ability to adapt and improve in the face of adversity.

59
Chris Paul.

Known for his exceptional basketball skills, he is a player who initially didn't dream of shining on the courts.

Born on May 6, 1985, in Winston-Salem, North Carolina, Paul was raised in a close-knit, hardworking family.

Despite his current fame as one of the best point guards in NBA history, basketball wasn't always his favorite sport.

During his youth, Chris was passionate about football, even though he didn't have the typical physical build for the sport.

His tenacity led him to actively participate on the football team, although his path eventually shifted toward basketball.

Upon entering high school at West Forsyth High School, Paul was practically forced to join the basketball team, a sport that initially didn't interest him.

However, over time, he developed an undeniable love and talent for the game.

Within two years, he became a key star for his team, proving that his place was on the basketball courts, not the football fields.

His skill and work ethic soon catapulted him to the national stage, and the rest is history

In his professional career, Chris Paul has been selected to participate in the NBA All-Star Game eight times, an achievement reserved for the league's most outstanding players.

His game has been characterized by his exceptional vision, his ability to assist his teammates, and his leadership both on and off the court.

Although he began his professional career with the New Orleans Hornets, he is widely known for his time with the Los Angeles Clippers, where he became the central piece of the team.

Throughout his career, Paul has been given various nicknames, including "CP3," "Cowboy," "Cipher Pol," "The Storm," and "Assassin."

Each of these nicknames reflects a different facet of his personality and playing style on the court.

One of the most poignant stories in Chris Paul's life is that of his grandfather, known as "Papa Chilly."

This man, who was a central figure in Paul's life, was brutally murdered in 2002 during a robbery at his home.

Devastated by the loss, Chris decided to honor his grandfather in a unique way.

In a basketball game shortly after his death, Paul scored exactly 61 points, one for each year of his grandfather's life.

Then, in a symbolic gesture, he deliberately missed a free throw and asked to be substituted, leaving everyone with a powerful lesson of love and respect for his family.

Chris Paul is also a great admirer of legendary players such as Allen Iverson, Magic Johnson, and Michael Jordan, who inspired him to perfect his game and reach great heights in his career.

Although he started as a fan of the Chicago Bulls and the Carolina Panthers, Paul became a fundamental pillar of the teams he has played for, including the New Orleans Hornets, Los Angeles Clippers, Houston Rockets, Oklahoma City Thunder, Phoenix Suns, and currently the Golden State Warriors.

Throughout his career, Chris Paul has demonstrated that he is not only an elite player but also a man of strong principles and values.

His dedication to the sport and his love for his family have made him a figure admired both on and off the court.

60

Tracy Lamar McGrady, Jr.

Born on May 24, 1979, in Bartow, Florida, is a former basketball player who left an indelible mark on the NBA.

Recognized for his skill and playing style, McGrady was one of the most outstanding players of his generation.

However, his life is full of curiosities and interesting aspects that go beyond his career on the court.

McGrady grew up in Auburndale, Florida, in a family with an unconventional structure.

His father was not very present in his life, so he was primarily raised by his mother, Melanise Williford, and his grandmother.

His childhood was marked by closeness to his family, and his aunt nicknamed him "Pumpkinhead," a name that quickly spread throughout his community.

A curious fact about Tracy is that he is a distant cousin of Vince Carter, another iconic NBA player.

Their grandmothers were first cousins, making them distant relatives.

This family connection was significant in their careers, as both shared the court on the Toronto Raptors, forming one of the most exciting duos in the league at the time.

During his school years, McGrady was not an exemplary student.

He started playing basketball at Auburndale High School, but he was expelled from the team in his junior year after an incident with a teacher, reflecting his rebellious and defiant character.

Despite his talent in basketball, Tracy did not excel academically and was considered lazy by many of his teachers.

In addition to his basketball career, McGrady has proven to be a businessman with diverse interests.

He is a co-owner of two companies: "Blue04," a bottled water company, and "Dasdak," a company that offers technology solutions and consulting.

Dasdak has significant sponsors like Microsoft, Toyota, and the New Orleans Pelicans, reflecting McGrady's success off the court.

From a young age, Tracy had a strong attraction to baseball, a sport he practiced alongside basketball.

After retiring from the NBA, he decided to try his hand at professional baseball, although his debut in the sport could have come much earlier, during the NBA lockout in 1998.

However, he chose not to enter MLB at that time, preferring to focus on his basketball career, which solidified after he fell in love with the sport at age 8 when he watched Anfernee "Penny" Hardaway play.

One of the most admirable aspects of Tracy McGrady is his commitment to humanitarian causes.

He traveled to a refugee camp in Chad, where he was deeply impacted by the living conditions of the refugees.

This journey motivated him to get involved in promoting collaboration agreements between American schools and colleges in Africa.

In 2009, McGrady starred in a documentary about these refugee camps, aiming to raise awareness about the difficult situation they face.

Regarding his personal life, McGrady is a deeply religious person.

He has Psalm 37 from the Bible tattooed on his right arm, which begins with the phrase, 'Do not fret because of evildoers, nor be envious of those who do wrong.'

This verse reflects his faith and philosophy of life, focused on trusting in God and not being disturbed by adversities.

After a 16-year career in the NBA, McGrady decided to retire from professional basketball, leaving behind a legacy that has established him as one of the great stars of the sport.

61

Dennis Rodman.

Born on May 13, 1961, in Trenton, New Jersey, he is one of the most iconic and controversial players in NBA history.

Known both for his defensive and rebounding skills and for his eccentric personality off the court, Rodman left an indelible mark on basketball and popular culture.

His life is full of curiosities, anecdotes, and surprising moments that have made him a fascinating figure.

Despite his success in the NBA, Rodman's beginnings in basketball were not promising.

During high school, he was only 1.68 meters tall and did not stand out in the sport.

However, he experienced a sudden growth spurt, reaching 2.01 meters, which motivated him to give basketball another chance.

With perseverance and hard work, Rodman transformed his game and became a master of rebounding and defense, qualities that took him to the NBA elite.

Rodman is known for his extravagant lifestyle, which includes numerous famous partners and behavior always in the media spotlight.

He was briefly married to actress Carmen Electra and had a relationship with singer Madonna, who reportedly encouraged him to have a child with her to "create a superchild."

Additionally, Rodman has never hidden his sexuality, even claiming that he has had sexual relations in every room of the Berto Center, the Chicago Bulls' training facility.

This behavior, though scandalous, is part of Rodman's legacy as a figure without limits and without regrets.

In 2010, during a party at the Hamptons Hotel, Rodman created an embarrassing moment when, after repeatedly taking the microphone to entertain guests, he retired to his room with six women, forgetting to return the microphone.

This caused the attendees to inadvertently hear his private conversation, creating quite a stir.

Besides his basketball career, Rodman explored other facets like wrestling and acting.

In 1997, he debuted in World Championship Wrestling (WCW), where he had several matches, though with little success.

He also appeared on television and in movies, notably in the series "3rd Rock from the Sun" and the film "Double Team" alongside Jean-Claude Van Damme.

He even lent his voice to a character in the video game "Dead or Alive Xtreme Beach Volleyball" in 2003.

Throughout his career, Rodman won five NBA championships and established himself as one of the best defenders and rebounders in basketball history.

However, his legacy goes beyond his achievements on the court.

He is a figure who challenged norms both within and outside of sports, becoming a counterculture icon and a character who will always be remembered for his authenticity and indomitable spirit.

62

Anfernee "Penny" Hardaway.

Born on July 18, 1971, in Memphis, Tennessee, he is a basketball legend who left an indelible mark on the NBA during the 1990s.

Standing 2.10 meters tall and possessing versatile skills that allowed him to play both shooting guard and point guard, Hardaway was one of the most outstanding players of his era.

Although his career was cut short by injuries, his talent and charisma made him a basketball icon.

Here are some of the most notable curiosities about Anfernee Hardaway that you may not have known.

Hardaway was a leader in triple-doubles during his career.

In April 2003, he achieved a triple-double with 10 rebounds, 10 assists, and 10 points, along with 2 blocks and 3 steals.

This feat reaffirmed his ability to impact the game in multiple facets.

Additionally, to this day, he holds the record for the best steals average in Orlando Magic history, with an average of 1.9 per game.

Hardaway's career was recognized from the beginning.

In 1993, Sports Illustrated magazine compared him to legends like Magic Johnson, George Gervin, Julius Erving, Pete Maravich, and Scottie Pippen, highlighting his unique combination of skills.

Michael Jordan, considered by many to be the greatest player of all time, even said that Hardaway "has more talent than I ever had," which underscores the level of respect and admiration that Hardaway generated among his peers.

One of the most iconic aspects of Hardaway was his association with Nike, and his line of sneakers, the "Penny Hardaway Sneakers," became a hit among basketball fans.

To promote the brand, Nike created a puppet named "Lil Penny," a miniature and humorous version of Hardaway.

Lil Penny, voiced by comedian Chris Rock, appeared in several memorable commercials that contributed to Hardaway's popularity off the court.

It's worth noting that despite his immense talent, Hardaway's career was marred by injuries. After Michael Jordan's first retirement in 1993, many believed that Hardaway would be his natural successor as the face of the NBA.

However, continuous injuries, especially to his knees, prevented him from reaching the superstar status that many had anticipated.

Although he didn't achieve his full potential, his impact on the game and his style are still fondly remembered by fans.

A fun fact about Hardaway is the origin of his nickname, "Penny." His grandmother gave him this nickname, saying that he was "pretty as a penny."

The Southern pronunciation of "pretty" as "penny" led everyone to start calling him that, and the nickname stuck with him throughout his life and career.

63

Chris Webber.

Born on March 1, 1973, in Detroit, Michigan, he is one of the most memorable figures in the NBA.

For 15 years, his presence on the court was synonymous with spectacle, standing out for his versatility and skill both in the paint and in ball distribution.

Webber was not only a talented power forward, but his creative and technical style of play made him a unique player, impossible to imitate.

Although his career was marked by successes and accolades, it was also accompanied by lesser-known curiosities.

One interesting aspect of Chris Webber's life is his love for dogs. He owns two Rottweilers named Zeek and Zora, whom he considers a fundamental part of his life.

Moreover, Webber is not just a basketball player; he is also a psychology graduate from the University of Michigan, demonstrating his interest in the human mind and his analytical abilities—traits that likely contributed to his on-court intelligence.

For three years, Webber was at the center of tabloid attention due to his relationship with the famous model Tyra Banks.

Their relationship was one of the most talked-about topics in the media, making him a recurring figure in entertainment magazines.

In addition to his NBA career, Webber ventured into the music industry.

He produced a song on the album "Hip Hop Is Dead" by rapper Nas, showcasing his versatility and passion for the arts.

This wasn't his only foray into music; in February 1999, Webber released his own album titled "Much Drama", revealing another creative side of his personality.

Webber has also shown a strong affinity for water sports, which he practices whenever his free time allows.

This passion for the water complements his approach to maintaining a balanced and active lifestyle off the court.

In 1995, Webber made a brief appearance on the television series "New York Undercover", highlighting his interest in exploring different fields beyond basketball.

Despite his undeniable talent and remarkable career, many experts believe that Webber's career could have been even more brilliant if not for injuries.

These injuries, which affected him at key moments in his career, prevented him from reaching his full potential in the NBA.

Even so, Webber is considered a brilliant player, and his legacy continues to be admired in the basketball world.

64

Kawhi Leonard.

Born on June 29, 1991, in Los Angeles, California, he is one of the most outstanding and enigmatic players in the NBA.

Standing 2.01 meters tall, Leonard has established himself as a versatile forward, known for both his offensive capabilities and his formidable defense.

Since his early days in the league, he has captured the attention of fans and critics alike with his work ethic, focus on the game, and reserved demeanor off the court.

Kawhi Leonard is an example of dedication and study of the game.

During an injury that kept him off the court, he developed the habit of meticulously analyzing his strengths and weaknesses, as well as those of his teammates and opponents.

This meticulous approach not only allowed him to improve his own game but also to find ways to counter his opponents, which has been key to his development as one of the most complete players in the NBA.

In 2016, Leonard was selected for the NBA All-Star Game for the first time, a recognition of his growing influence in the league.

However, his path to NBA stardom began with an unexpected twist.

He was selected in the 2011 draft by the Indiana Pacers, but before making his debut with the team, he was traded to the San Antonio Spurs.

This move proved to be crucial for his career, as under the guidance of Gregg Popovich and surrounded by veterans like Tim Duncan, Tony Parker, and Manu Ginóbili, Leonard quickly evolved.

One of the most notable aspects of Kawhi Leonard is his nickname "The Claw," which comes from the extraordinary size of his hands.

With a wingspan of 28.6 centimeters from fingertip to fingertip, his hands are larger than a basketball, which has a diameter of 24 centimeters.

These hands give him a significant advantage in ball handling and defense, allowing him to make steals, rebounds, and blocks exceptionally well.

Beyond his imposing physicality, Leonard's success is attributed to his dedication and constant desire to improve.

He is known for his reserved nature and focus on the game, avoiding the media spotlight that accompanies many of his contemporaries.

This focus, combined with his skill on both ends of the court, has made him one of the most respected players in the NBA.

65

Kyrie Irving.

He is a talented basketball player born on March 23, 1992, in Melbourne, Australia, though he grew up in New Jersey, United States.

Standing 1.91 meters tall and possessing impressive skills on the court, Irving quickly catapulted to NBA stardom.

He was selected as the first overall pick in the 2011 draft by the Cleveland Cavaliers, becoming the second Australian-born player to be chosen first in an NBA draft, following Andrew Bogut.

One of the most fascinating aspects of Kyrie Irving's life is his deep fandom for the Brooklyn Nets.

Although he began his professional career with the Cleveland Cavaliers, his emotional connection to the Nets dates back to his childhood in New Jersey, where the team, then known as the New Jersey Nets, inspired him to pursue basketball.

This fandom eventually led him to join the Brooklyn Nets in 2019, fulfilling a childhood dream.

Kyrie Irving is also known for his alter ego "Uncle Drew," a character he portrays in a series of commercials for Pepsi.

In these ads, Irving transforms into an elderly man who surprises young players on the basketball courts with his incredible skill.

This character became so popular that in 2018, he became the star of a sports comedy film titled "Uncle Drew", in which Irving continued to portray the charismatic elderly basketball player.

In his NBA career, Kyrie developed a special relationship with LeBron James when they both played for the Cleveland Cavaliers.

Together, they led the team to multiple NBA Finals, culminating in the historic 2016 championship, where the Cavaliers came back from a 3-1 deficit to defeat the Golden State Warriors.

The friendship and on-court chemistry between Kyrie and LeBron became a central story for the team and the league during that time.

Kyrie's father, Drederick Irving, has been a constant and powerful influence in his life.

After the tragic death of his mother when Kyrie was only four years old, his father took on the role of mentor and guide.

Drederick, who was also a standout basketball player in his youth, instilled in Kyrie a love for the sport and the value of hard work.

In a touching act of gratitude, Kyrie has given all the trophies and medals he has won, including his 2016 NBA championship ring, to his father as a symbol of appreciation for all the sacrifices he made for him.

In addition to his NBA career, Kyrie has been a complex and sometimes controversial figure off the court, as he has expressed beliefs and opinions that have sparked debate, such as his claim that the Earth is flat, although he later clarified that his comments were misunderstood.

66

Michael Carter-Williams.

He is an American basketball player born on October 10, 1991, in Hamilton, Massachusetts.

Standing 1.98 meters tall, he plays as a point guard and has been recognized for his defensive ability, versatility, and ball-handling skills.

Throughout his career, he has played for several NBA teams, initially standing out for his impressive rookie season.

One of the most memorable moments of Carter-Williams' career was his NBA debut with the Philadelphia 76ers.

In his first game, he set a historic record by becoming the player with the most steals in a debut game, totaling 9 steals.

This achievement was particularly significant as it placed him in a prestigious position alongside legends like Shaquille O'Neal, who had been the last rookie to make such an immediate impact in the league since 1992.

During his rookie season, Carter-Williams averaged 17.2 points, 7.3 assists, 5.3 rebounds, and 2.92 steals per game, leading him to be named Eastern Conference Rookie of the Month multiple times.

In 2014, Carter-Williams was awarded the Rookie of the Year title and was included in the NBA All-Rookie First Team, a distinction that placed him alongside names like Oscar Robertson and Magic Johnson.

These achievements highlighted his versatility and ability to influence multiple aspects of the game, making him one of the few players to average 16-6-6 in their rookie season.

An interesting aspect of Carter-Williams' career was his trade to the Chicago Bulls in 2016, where he was exchanged for Tony Snell.

During his transition to the team, there was speculation about whether he would wear the number 1 jersey, which previously belonged to Derrick Rose.

However, he chose to wear the number 7, an iconic number for the Bulls due to the legacy of Toni Kukoc, a legendary sixth man for the team.

In 2016, Carter-Williams faced a significant setback when he suffered a torn labrum in his left hip, which required surgery in March of that year.

This injury sidelined him for the season, but a full recovery was expected within three months.

Despite his passion for basketball, Carter-Williams also has an interest in baseball, though his skill in this sport is not as remarkable.

A humorous incident occurred during a Milwaukee Brewers game, where Carter-Williams was invited to throw a ceremonial first pitch.

However, his throw ended in a mishap when the ball hit a television camera, eliciting laughter from the spectators and revealing that his baseball skills were not on par with his basketball abilities.

67

Tony Parker.

Born as William Anthony Parker on May 17, 1982, in Bruges, Belgium, he is a former professional basketball player known for his speed, skills, and leadership on the court.

Although born in Belgium, he was raised in France, where he developed his career and became one of the most iconic players in European basketball and the NBA.

Throughout his life, Parker has accumulated a series of anecdotes and curiosities that have marked both his professional career and personal life.

Tony Parker grew up in a household with a strong sports influence.

His father, Tony Parker Sr., was a former basketball player who had played at the University of Chicago before moving to Europe.

It was in France where he met Tony's mother, Pamela Firestone, a former model.

Despite being surrounded by basketball, young Tony initially gravitated towards soccer.

However, after witnessing the impact Michael Jordan had on the basketball world, he decided to shift his focus and dedicated himself to basketball at the age of 15, standing out as a talented point guard due to his speed and leadership abilities.

In 1999, Parker began his professional career with Paris Basket Racing in France, where he played for two seasons before making the leap to the NBA.

He was selected as the 28th pick in the 2001 NBA Draft by the San Antonio Spurs.

He quickly established himself as the team's starting point guard, forming a formidable trio alongside Tim Duncan and Manu Ginóbili.

With the Spurs, Parker won four NBA championships (2003, 2005, 2007, and 2014) and was named Finals MVP in 2007, becoming the first European player to receive this honor.

In addition to his basketball career, Tony Parker has explored other interests, such as music; he released a self-titled album in 2007, showcasing his versatility and passion for the arts.

More recently, he has started taking piano lessons, suggesting that music may continue to play an important role in his life after retirement.

Parker is also a passionate advocate for animals and a cat lover, reflecting his sensitive side and his aversion to animal cruelty.

Additionally, he is an active philanthropist, being a member of the "Make-A-Wish Foundation," which works to fulfill the wishes of children with terminal illnesses.

In his personal life, Tony Parker was married to actress Eva Longoria, famous for her role in "Desperate Housewives".

However, the couple divorced in 2010 amid rumors of infidelity on Parker's part.

After the divorce, Parker continued his personal and professional life successfully, remaining a prominent figure both in basketball and in other areas.

Throughout his career, Tony Parker was selected six times to participate in the NBA All-Star Game and was instrumental in the internationalization of French basketball.

His impact on European basketball is immeasurable, and he has inspired a generation of French players to follow in his footsteps in the NBA.

Additionally, Parker owns 20% of the shares of the French basketball club ASVEL Lyon-Villeurbanne, demonstrating his commitment to the sport even after his retirement as a player.

68

Terrence James Elijah Ross.

Born on February 2, 1991, in Portland, Oregon, he is a prominent basketball player who has made his mark in the NBA.

Standing at 1.98 meters, Ross has been known for his scoring ability, particularly from beyond the three-point line.

Ross was selected as the eighth overall pick in the 2012 NBA Draft by the Toronto Raptors.

From his early years in the league, Ross demonstrated his scoring ability, especially in crucial games.

One of his most surprising achievements occurred on January 25, 2014, when he scored 51 points in a game against the Los Angeles Clippers.

What makes this feat remarkable is that he accomplished it while averaging less than 10 points per game that season, making him the first and only player in NBA history to score 50 points in a game with such a low average.

One of the most notable victories in his career was winning the NBA Slam Dunk Contest in 2013 during All-Star Weekend in Houston, Texas.

His victory in this contest solidified his reputation as a player with exceptional athletic ability and a great sense of showmanship.

His final dunk, which replicated Vince Carter's famous "360 between the legs," left a lasting impression on fans and earned him the championship.

Basketball is more than just a sport for Ross; it's a path he has traveled with the unconditional support of his family, especially his mother.

After his historic 51-point performance against the Clippers, Ross decided to keep the game ball as a priceless keepsake.

In a touching gesture, he chose to give that ball to his mother, thanking her for her constant support and for being a source of inspiration in his life.

Like every player, Ross has faced his share of ups and downs.

In one game, he attempted a "windmill dunk," a spectacular move that involves dunking the ball with one hand while running towards the basket.

However, he missed, leading to an awkward moment, but Ross didn't let this setback affect him, and in the same game, he redeemed himself with an impressive 360° dunk that brought the crowd to its feet.

In 2017, Ross was traded to the Orlando Magic, where he continued to prove his worth as a "floor-spacing wing," a player specialized in spacing the floor with his ability to score from the three-point line.

Throughout his career, Ross has also dealt with injuries, such as the one to his left thumb during a practice, which sidelined him for an indefinite period.

Despite these challenges, his determination and dedication to basketball have helped him recover and keep moving forward.

69

Shaquille O'Neal.

He is one of the most iconic and dominant players in NBA history.

His career in the league, which spanned over 19 years, was filled with achievements both on and off the court.

Here are some of the most notable curiosities about "Shaq," illustrating his impact on basketball and popular culture.

Shaquille O'Neal is known for having a large number of nicknames throughout his career.

Some of these include "Shaq," "The Big Aristotle," "The Diesel," "Superman," "The Big Cactus," and "The Big Shamrock."

Interestingly, many of these nicknames were created by himself, showcasing his wit and sense of humor.

Shaq always had great self-confidence and a magnetic personality, which made him one of the most beloved and recognizable players in NBA history.

As a child, O'Neal was a huge fan of Spider-Man, his favorite superhero.

His admiration was so great that he tried to emulate the web-slinger's stunts when he was young.

On one occasion, Shaq decided to jump from a tree, believing he could imitate his hero.

However, reality hit him hard when he ended up breaking both of his wrists.

This anecdote shows the energy and bravery (or recklessness) that Shaquille had even before becoming a basketball superstar.

Shaquille O'Neal attended Louisiana State University (LSU), where he stood out as one of the best college players of his generation.

During his time at LSU, Shaq broke numerous records and earned the admiration of both his teammates and fans.

In recognition of his legacy, he was inducted into the university's Hall of Fame, an honor that reflects his lasting impact on college basketball.

Shaquille O'Neal not only excelled in basketball but also ventured into music.

In the early 1990s, he launched his career as a rapper with the album *Shaq Diesel,* which was a commercial success.

The album achieved Platinum certification, an impressive accomplishment for an athlete turned musician.

This success demonstrated that Shaq had talent and charisma not only on the court but also in the entertainment world.

In his NBA career, Shaquille O'Neal established himself as one of the most dominant players of all time.

He was selected 15 times for the All-Star Game and won four NBA championships: three with the Los Angeles Lakers and one with the Miami Heat.

His size, strength, and ability to play in the post made him a true phenomenon in the league.

In 2016, he was inducted into the Basketball Hall of Fame, an honor that celebrates his impact on the sport.

Throughout his career and personal life, Shaquille O'Neal has been a model of positive behavior.

Despite living a life filled with luxury and fame, Shaq has avoided scandals and remained focused on his career and family.

His dedication to basketball and his influence on popular culture have made him an icon, not only for sports fans but also for those seeking an example of success and perseverance.

70

Rudy Gay.

Born in Baltimore, Maryland, he is a prominent basketball player who has made his mark in the NBA since entering the league.

From his early days in the NBA, Rudy Gay has been highly valued for his versatility on the court.

His ability to play both as a small forward and power forward has made him a sought-after asset for many teams.

Throughout his career, he has been known for his consistent scoring ability and his defensive skills, which have made him stand out in the league.

Rudy Gay has been one of the most sought-after players in the NBA, especially during free agency periods.

His talent and ability to change the course of a game have made him a target for several teams looking to strengthen their rosters.

Despite receiving numerous offers over the years, Gay has maintained high standards for his value, rejecting offers he did not consider commensurate with his level of play.

This has allowed him to remain a high-profile player in the league.

In January 2017, Rudy Gay suffered a severe Achilles tendon injury while playing for the Sacramento Kings.

This injury was a significant blow to his career, as it required surgery and sidelined him for the season.

The injury was particularly challenging because it occurred just as his contract with the Kings was about to expire, creating uncertainty about his future in the NBA.

However, Gay demonstrated resilience by recovering and continuing his career in the league.

Throughout his career, Rudy Gay has had some conflicts with coaches, particularly with Vlade Divac, who was his coach with the Sacramento Kings.

The tensions between them stemmed from the perception that Gay was reserved and did not always openly communicate his thoughts or concerns.

These differences led to rumors of a possible trade involving Gay, though he ultimately stayed with the team until he decided to explore free agency.

Off the court, Rudy Gay has been recognized for his commitment to the community.

In 2016, he was named NBA Cares Community Assist Player of the Month and Hoops Ambassador by St. Jude Children's Research Hospital.

Gay donated $20,000 to the program and supported the initiative by encouraging donors to pledge a certain amount of money for every point he scored.

Additionally, he has personally donated a total of $22 million to the hospital, demonstrating his dedication to charitable causes and his desire to make a difference in the lives of others.

71

Nate Robinson.

Nate Robinson is a former NBA player who left an indelible mark on the basketball world thanks to his incredible athletic ability, particularly his skill in jumping and executing spectacular dunks, despite his short stature.

Throughout his career, Robinson proved that size is not a barrier to success in the NBA.

Standing at just 1.75 meters, Robinson ranks among the shortest players in the league's history.

However, he used his size as an advantage, standing out for his speed, agility, and astonishing jumping ability.

His skill in performing impressive dunks allowed him to win the NBA Slam Dunk Contest three times (2006, 2009, and 2010), a record he shares with the legendary Dominique Wilkins.

Coming from a family of athletes, Nate Robinson inherited his love for sports from his father, Jacque Robinson, who was a standout football player and MVP in the Rose Bowl and Orange Bowl in 1982 and 1985, respectively.

Nate also played football in his youth and showed great talent in the sport before deciding to focus on basketball.

Despite many believing that his height would be a hindrance to success in basketball, Robinson defied all expectations.

He chose a sport where height is traditionally favored and dominated it with his natural talent, his ability to jump, and an unbreakable determination.

Robinson not only made it to the NBA but also had a standout career, playing for several teams, including the New York Knicks, Chicago Bulls, and Boston Celtics.

In 2009, during the NBA Slam Dunk Contest, Nate Robinson faced off against Dwight Howard, known as "Superman" for his imposing physique and skills on the court.

In one of the most memorable dunks in the contest's history, Robinson literally jumped over Howard, winning the contest and earning the nickname "Kryptonite," a reference to the only element capable of weakening Superman.

From an early age, Robinson showed an interest in the world of entertainment.

At one point in his career, there were rumors that Spike Lee, the renowned film director, was considering giving him a role in one of his movies.

Although this never materialized, Robinson confessed that he is a big Disney fan and has always dreamed of lending his voice to an animated character.

His favorite movie is "Toy Story", reflecting his more childlike and dreamy side.

Nate Robinson experienced a personal tragedy when his younger brother, Deron Isiah Robinson, passed away due to Sudden Infant Death Syndrome (SIDS) on May 21, 1997.

This painful event deeply affected him, and in tribute to his brother, Nate had his name tattooed on his left bicep.

Before every game, Robinson touches this tattoo, paying an emotional tribute to his brother.

After his successful NBA career, Nate Robinson has considered returning to football, the sport he also excelled in during his youth.

Although his main focus has been basketball, his athletic ability and passion for sports have led him to explore new opportunities, demonstrating that he is a truly versatile athlete.

Nate Robinson is an example of how determination and passion can overcome any obstacle.

His story inspires many to pursue their dreams, no matter what others may say or think.

72

Allen Iverson.

Nicknamed "The Answer," he is one of the most iconic and controversial figures in NBA history.

Born on June 7, 1975, in Hampton, Virginia, Iverson left an indelible mark on basketball, not only for his skill on the court but also for his unique personality and a life filled with ups and downs.

Iverson had a difficult childhood, marked by poverty and legal troubles.

Despite these challenges, his talent in sports was undeniable, excelling in both football and basketball during high school.

However, his career was jeopardized when he was arrested at the age of 17 after a fight at a bowling alley, an incident that led to a 15-year prison sentence, although he served only four months before the conviction was overturned due to a lack of clear evidence.

After his release, Iverson was given a second chance at Georgetown University, where he played under coach John Thompson and quickly established himself as a star, winning two Big East Defensive Player of the Year awards before declaring for the 1996 NBA draft.

Iverson was selected as the first overall pick in the 1996 NBA Draft by the Philadelphia 76ers.

From his first game, Iverson demonstrated his scoring ability, averaging 23.5 points per game in his rookie season and winning the Rookie of the Year award.

During his NBA career, Iverson was known for his speed, ball-handling skills, and ability to score at any moment, despite his relatively short stature (1.83 meters).

One of the most memorable moments of his career occurred in his rookie season when he crossed over Michael Jordan, leaving him on the floor—a moment that symbolized a generational shift in the NBA.

Iverson was also known for his aggressive style of play, which allowed him to lead the league in scoring for four seasons.

The nickname "The Answer" was self-imposed by Iverson and reflects his belief that basketball was the answer to all the difficulties and challenges he faced in his life.

To him, basketball was more than just a sport; it was his escape and salvation.

Iverson not only impacted the NBA with his game but also with his style.

He was one of the first players to popularize the use of baggy clothes, braids, and a significant number of tattoos in the league, challenging the norms of the time and helping to transform NBA culture.

His influence extended beyond the court, impacting fashion and music, particularly in hip-hop culture.

Throughout his life, Iverson also faced various legal issues, financial problems, and personal challenges.

His NBA career was marked by multiple conflicts with coaches and team management, especially with the Philadelphia 76ers.

He also faced criticism for his attitude towards practice, highlighted by his famous press conference where he repeatedly said, "We're talking about practice" when questioned about missing a training session.

Throughout his career, Iverson was an 11-time NBA All-Star, won the Most Valuable Player (MVP) award in 2001, and led the 76ers to the NBA Finals that same year.

Despite not winning a championship, Iverson is considered one of the best shooting guards in NBA history.

In 2013, Iverson officially retired from professional basketball.

In 2014, the Philadelphia 76ers retired his jersey number 3 in his honor, immortalizing his legacy with the franchise.

In addition to his basketball career, Iverson also ventured into the music world.

In 2000, he released a rap album titled "40 Bars" under the stage name "Jewelz."

However, the album generated controversy due to its explicit lyrics and was never officially released.

73

Hakeem Abdul Olajuwon.

Also known as "Akeem" in the early years of his career, he is one of the greatest players in NBA history.

Hailing from Nigeria, Olajuwon played for the Houston Rockets for 15 seasons, leaving an indelible legacy before retiring in 2002.

Recognized for his extraordinary skill on the court, Olajuwon stood out as a great team player, perfecting a set of fakes and moves under the basket that made him a true master of the low post.

One of the most impressive milestones of his career is that he is one of the few players in NBA history to achieve a quadruple-double, a feat that highlights his multifaceted impact on the game.

One of the most memorable moments of Olajuwon's career was his triple-double feat with 12 blocks, 24 points, and 21 rebounds in a game where the Rockets defeated the Utah Jazz 100 to 82, 27 years ago.

This performance exemplifies his dominance on both ends of the court, demonstrating his ability to influence the game both defensively and offensively.

In 1991, Olajuwon converted to Islam, which led to a change in his name from "Akeem" to "Hakeem."

His faith played a central role in his life, and he had the habit of reading the Quran before and after each game.

However, after his retirement, he had an incident with U.S. authorities when he attempted to establish a mosque in the United States, which led to an investigation for alleged terrorist activity, although no evidence was found against him.

Before dedicating himself to basketball, Olajuwon played soccer in his native Nigeria, where he was a goalkeeper, and also enjoyed playing handball.

It wasn't until he was 15 years old that he became interested in basketball, a sport in which he would become a global legend.

His experience as a soccer goalkeeper contributed to his agility and reflexes on the court, skills that he uniquely applied to basketball.

One of Olajuwon's most famous moves is the "Dream Shake", a fake-and-turn hook shot that is nearly impossible to stop.

This move has become one of the most iconic in the NBA, and many players, including LeBron James, Kobe Bryant, Kenneth Faried, and Yao Ming, have sought to learn it directly from him.

Olajuwon organizes intensive training camps during the summer, where he teaches his techniques to professional players who want to improve their post-game.

74

Ricky Rubio

Born in El Masnou, Spain, he is a talented basketball player known for his skills as a point guard, his court vision, and his ability to make precise assists.

Standing at 1.93 meters tall with a fair complexion, Rubio is one of the most recognized and respected players of his generation, currently playing for the Minnesota Timberwolves in the NBA.

Rubio had an exceptional start to his sports career.

At the age of 14, he became the youngest player to debut in the ACB League, the top basketball league in Spain.

This achievement was made possible by the vision of coach Aito García Reneses, who saw special talent in Rubio and invited him to train with the ACB team, La Penya.

This was a decisive moment in Rubio's life, marking the beginning of his professional career.

His transition to the NBA was not without challenges, as when he entered the NBA draft, he still had an active contract with Club Joventut de Badalona.

This contract required Rubio to pay a considerable sum to be released, leading the young player to negotiate and eventually take the case to court.

Although an agreement was ultimately reached between the Spanish club and the Minnesota Timberwolves, Rubio chose to accept an offer from FC Barcelona, delaying his entry into the NBA for a few years.

This decision was partly motivated by the generous contract of 3.7 million euros offered by the Catalan club, as well as the comfort of staying in Spain for a bit longer.

Rubio is known not only for his skill on the court but also for his sincerity and openness about his personal life.

He has spoken openly about his fears and dreams, admitting that he fears injuries and hopes to stay healthy throughout his career.

He has also shared his desire to find love and start a family in the future.

One of the most curious anecdotes from his childhood reveals his admiration for Michael Jordan.

When he was young, after being asked by his teacher what he wanted to be when he grew up, Rubio responded that he wanted to be Black because he associated that trait with greatness in basketball, inspired by his idol, Jordan.

This innocent and sincere response reflects his passion for basketball from an early age.

Today, Ricky Rubio is recognized for his ability to generate assists, lead the game from the point guard position, and contribute significantly to his teams.

His combination of talent, humility, and dedication has made him a beloved figure both in Spain and the NBA, and he continues to make his mark in the world of basketball.

75

Kevin Garnett.

He is one of the most iconic players in NBA history, known not only for his talent on the court but also for his intensity, character, and the stories surrounding his career.

Born on May 19, 1976, in Mauldin, South Carolina, Garnett left an indelible mark on professional basketball during his 21 years in the NBA, with an impact that goes beyond titles and statistics.

Garnett was drafted in 1995 straight out of high school, an uncommon move at the time, but one that proved to be a resounding success.

Throughout his career, he accumulated countless achievements, including the NBA MVP award in 2004 and an NBA championship with the Boston Celtics in 2008.

He was also named an All-Star 15 times and selected multiple times for the All-NBA and All-Defensive teams.

His versatility allowed him to excel both defensively and offensively, making him one of the most complete players in history.

One of the most famous curiosities about Kevin Garnett is his insistence on underestimating his own height.

Despite officially measuring 2.13 meters, Garnett always claimed to be 2.10 meters tall.

This was due to his aversion to being labeled as a center, as he preferred to play as a power forward, where he felt he could better utilize his skills on the perimeter.

Garnett was very aware of the implications of his height on the position he would be assigned on the team, and he fiercely defended his right to avoid being pigeonholed as a traditional "seven-footer."

Garnett's intensity is legendary.

On the court, he was known for his aggression and competitive mentality, which drove him to play every game as if it were his last.

However, this intensity wasn't limited to just the games.

Tyronn Lue, a close friend and former teammate, shared an anecdote that reflects how Garnett lived every moment with the same passion he brought to the court.

One afternoon at Garnett's house, while they were watching a TV show, Garnett became so excited watching a singing competition that he started yelling and sweating as if he were in a game, even going so far as to punch the wall out of frustration.

This level of intensity was something that defined him both on and off the court.

Garnett also had a strong sense of justice, something that accompanied him from a young age.

In his teenage years, while living in Mauldin, he was arrested several times in incidents that he and his family described as racially motivated.

These confrontations with local authorities shaped his character and made him more determined not to tolerate injustices, a trait that was reflected in his career and his leadership on the teams he played for.

76

Dwight Howard.

Nicknamed "Superman" for his incredible athletic ability and imposing presence on the court, he is a basketball player who has made a significant mark in the NBA.

In addition to being an outstanding center with numerous awards and achievements throughout his career, Howard is known for his jovial character and his quirky routines outside of basketball.

Since he was young, Howard has shown a childlike spirit and a great passion for movies, especially Disney films.

Among his favorites are "The Lion King" and "Finding Nemo", which he has repeatedly mentioned in interviews.

This love for animated films reflects his playful nature and his connection to his inner child, something that also manifests in his behavior both on and off the court.

Interestingly, one of his strategies for concentrating and improving his free-throw accuracy is singing Beyoncé songs.

Howard has confessed that the music of the iconic singer helps him find the calm and focus needed to turn his shots into points, adding a personal and unique touch to his game preparation.

From a very young age, Howard developed the habit of writing down his goals on a list and crossing off those he has achieved.

This ritual of setting goals and tracking his progress has been a fundamental part of his success.

Among the goals he wrote down as a child, one of the most important was being selected in the NBA draft, which he achieved, becoming one of the most dominant players of his generation.

His list of goals is a clear example of his determined focus and commitment to achieving his dreams.

In addition to his dedication to basketball, Howard is a man of deep religious faith.

Throughout his career, he has expressed his desire to use his platform as an NBA player to promote the Christian faith and glorify the name of God.

According to Howard, his success in sports would not have been possible without his faith, and he seeks to inspire others through his example and testimony.

Physically, Howard is also notable for his impressive size.

Standing at 2.11 meters tall, his shoe size is equally impressive, as he wears a size 18.

This detail makes him a true "bigfoot" on and off the court, further highlighting his physical presence.

Howard is truly a "miracle child," as his mother, Sheryl Howard, suffered seven miscarriages before conceiving him.

This fact has been a source of inspiration for him and his family, reinforcing his belief that his life is blessed and has a special purpose.

Regarding his pre-game rituals, Howard has a peculiar routine: spending 25 minutes in the bathroom before each game.

During this time, he focuses on reading, relaxing, and singing, which helps him clear his mind and mentally prepare for the game.

This habit is part of his relaxed and jovial approach to the sport, which contrasts with the intensity of the game.

In addition to his success on the court, Howard has shown an interest in acting and has proven to be a fun and charismatic character.

He is often seen impersonating figures like Shaquille O'Neal and Arnold Schwarzenegger, leading some to speculate about a possible future in acting.

However, despite criticism for his laid-back behavior, Howard remains true to himself, always smiling and enjoying every moment.

Printed in Dunstable, United Kingdom

76319809R00107